contentment

ALSO BY TRACY WILDE-PACE

Finding the Lost Art of Empathy:
Connecting Human to Human in a Disconnected World

contentment

The Sacred Path to
Loving the Life You Have

TRACY WILDE-PACE

HOWARD BOOKS

ATRIA

New York · London · Toronto · Sydney · New Delhi

HOWARD BOOKS

ATRIA

An Imprint of Simon & Schuster, Inc.
1230 Avenue of the Americas
New York, NY 10020

First Howard Books/Atria Books hardcover edition June 2021

HOWARD BOOKS/ATRIA BOOKS and colophon are trademarks of
Simon & Schuster, Inc.

For information about special discounts for bulk purchases, please contact Simon
& Schuster Special Sales at 1-866-506-1949 or business@simonandschuster.com.

The Simon & Schuster Speakers Bureau can bring authors to your live event. For
more information or to book an event, contact the Simon & Schuster Speakers
Bureau at 1-866-248-3049 or visit our website at www.simonspeakers.com.

Interior design by Timothy Shaner, NightandDayDesign.biz

Manufactured in the United States of America

1 3 5 7 9 10 8 6 4 2

Library of Congress Cataloging-in-Publication Data

Names: Wilde, Tracy, author.
Title: Contentment : the sacred path to loving the life you have /
Tracy Wilde-Pace.
Identifiers: LCCN 2020049529 (print) | LCCN 2020049530 (ebook) |
ISBN 9781501156311 | ISBN 9781501156328 (ebook)
Subjects: LCSH: Contentment—Religious aspects—Christianity.
Classification: LCC BV4647.C7 W54 2021 (print) | LCC BV4647.C7
(ebook) | DDC 248.4—dc23
LC record available at https://lccn.loc.gov/2020049529
LC ebook record available at https://lccn.loc.gov/2020049530

ISBN 978-1-5011-5631-1
ISBN 978-1-5011-5632-8 (ebook)

Page 215 constitutes a continuation of the copyright page.

This book is dedicated to my husband, Garrison.
I've heard it said the best things in life are worth waiting for
and you were well worth the wait!
I'm so honored to be your wife.

Contents

Chapter 1

What Is Contentment?
Already Not Yet

To me, there's nothing more frustrating than wanting to be home after a long trip overseas. A few years ago, I was returning home from Kenya to Idaho after teaching at the beautiful Kenya College of Ministry, which trains local pastors in practical ministry to help them build healthy, thriving churches. Every trip is unbelievably rewarding and so enjoyable! You've got to love that Kenyan tea! But after a few weeks of teaching all day, fighting mosquitoes, and trying to tame my wild, frizzy naturally curly hair, I was ready to head home.

This particular year I brought the greatest travel buddy ever with me, Vierra. Vierra is the quintessential international traveler. This girl is a legend and such an adventurer. She's traveled all over the world, so you don't have to worry about her handling the terrain of rocky roads or the unique local delicacies offered. Not to mention, she knows how to make you laugh.

But after a great few weeks with our lovely Kenyan pastors, both Vierra and I couldn't wait to get home. You know you're ready to go home when you leave for the airport way before you need to. I think we arrived a solid five hours before our flight was scheduled to depart, but we didn't mind one bit. We made our way to the airport lounge and settled in with free Wi-Fi and snacks. After a few hours of lounging, catching up on emails, and all things social media, we decided we should head for our gate since they would be boarding soon. Once we had arrived at the gate, we heard the news no traveler ever wants to hear: "Your flight has been delayed." Ugh. The worst. We felt like we had already been waiting for days. But, oh well. What are you going to do about it? So we settled in to the boarding area, and after another couple of hours waiting there, we finally heard the best news ever, which was "We'll be starting our boarding now." Praise the Lord! We're on our way now! Home is calling! It won't be long now.

Vierra and I comfortably nestle into our seats (as comfortably as you can in economy for a ten-hour flight) for the first leg of our journey home. Following a significant time for boarding and getting everyone seated, the pilot came on and said that air traffic control had delayed us. The pilot went on to say he wasn't sure how long the delay would be, but that he would get back to us as soon as he heard anything. Two hours later, we finally took off from Kenya, heading to Amsterdam. En route the flight attendants kept assuring the passengers that we wouldn't miss our connections and not to worry.

But worry is what I do best. So you bet I was worrying. Plus, I did the math in my head, and there was no way we were going to make our connection to the States with the already short layover that we had scheduled.

Sure enough, upon our arrival to Amsterdam, Vierra and I ran, tired, haggard-looking, through all the checkpoints to get to our gate, only to be told what we had already suspected: "You missed your flight."

We all have two options in these moments. One option is to freak out at the gate agent, who probably has about as much control over the delay and you missing your flight as you do over a two-year-old's temperament. So freaking out at the poor airline representative never seems like a great option. Or option two, to calmly accept the alternative plan the airline representative offers you and try to not let it ruin your life.

So Vierra and I chose the latter option and walked away, feeling a little dejected at the thought of being so close to, yet so far away from, home. We were smack-dab in the middle of two places. We weren't in Kenya anymore, but we still weren't home. Nevertheless, we chose to enjoy some extra time shopping at the airport and getting some coffee that, the closer we got to home, tasted more and more like American coffee.

By the time we arrived at our new gate and flight, we realized we had been going pretty long on this journey without a shower, brushed teeth, combed hair, or fresh clothes. We felt gross, and we looked gross! But remember, I told you, Vierra makes me laugh. So with all the inconveniences of the day, Vierra and I kept finding things to laugh about.

Just as we were getting ready to board the second leg of the trip, we heard, "Miss Wilde and Miss Reid, will you please see a gate agent?"

Vierra and I quickly jumped up from our seats and hurried to the first available gate agent, who told us we had been upgraded to business class due to the inconvenience of our previous flight and delay. Tears of joy welled up in my eyes, and I kept thanking the agent over and over. It was like the dam of our hearts broke open, and we began to share every little detail of our horrible journey with this kind person. At one point, I mentioned to her how awful it had been because look at how haggard we looked, to which the gate agent responded, "Yeah, like your hair," as she pointed at my hair with a look of both pity and compassion. Vierra and I roared in laughter. No one else would have been that bold to address my frizzy mane, which had increased in volume and frizz.

As we boarded and took our lush business class seats for the flight home, I recognized that being stuck between two moments isn't the worst thing in the world. However, it's always our goal to make it all the way home.

Have you ever felt stuck between two moments? As if you were almost somewhere but not quite there, and for whatever reason, you couldn't seem to get there? It's one of the most frustrating feelings to experience. We've all been there from time to time in our lives. You feel ready to be married, but there's no one even in sight. You feel so prepared to have children but struggle to conceive. You know you've worked overtime to get that promotion, but your boss doesn't seem to even know your name. It's a terrible feeling, stuck between wanting something and attaining it.

I'm learning that contentment is our true home. The journey to get there is not always easy, comfortable, or how we want it to look. Contentment is, in fact, not based on circumstances or the way we get there. Contentment is not the means to the end for true happiness and joy. Contentment is the end.

I believe at the bottom of every human soul is the deepest desire to be at home in contentment. The problem for most of us, however, is that we can't seem to find our way there. We get discouraged by every little and big disappointment in our lives. We seem only to be happy when the circumstances are just as they should be according to what we think or feel. We struggle into the depths of fear and anxiety, and we cannot even fathom feeling content in anything. It feels a whole lot like living in a perpetual *already not yet*.

This book is an attempt to help us all find our way back home to contentment. A place that doesn't need perfect circumstances or scenarios. In fact, home takes you as you are and helps you learn to build a life that is content no matter what life throws your way.

Together, I hope to explore how we can learn from what the Apostle Paul learned and knew when he said in Philippians 4:11, "Not that I am speaking of being in need, for I have learned in whatever situation I am to be content."[1] I have been so inspired by the life of Apostle Paul and his unwavering faith. A man who (as far as we know) was never married, ship-wrecked three times, put in prison on several accounts, and had numerous assassination attempts on his life. Yet he famously teaches us that no matter what life throws at you, you can learn to be content.

The thing about Paul is that before he was Paul the Apostle, he was Saul of Tarsus. Paul endured a long journey to become who we know and admire as the great Apostle Paul today. Saul of Tarsus was a young man raised in a strict Jewish tradition and thought and was devoted to the ancient traditions he was raised to follow. Saul and his contemporaries believed so vehemently that these codes were to be followed that they thought violence was justified if someone strayed from these strict traditions. Saul, likely, persecuted those who did not follow his beliefs. It is believed that Saul was in attendance and likely participated in the stoning death of Stephen. Stephen was one of the seven deacons chosen by the apostles in the early church to do the work of the ministry (see Acts 6). So how did Saul the persecutor become Paul the Apostle?

The short answer: a journey. The long answer will hopefully be unpacked throughout this book.

In Acts 9, Saul is walking along a road in Damascus when all of a sudden he encounters the God that he thought he was defending, but was actually persecuting. We have come to know this as the great Road to Damascus encounter. Certainly, this is the moment Paul receives a revelation of truth, and transformation follows. But Paul didn't become the Apostle overnight after this incredible face-to-face encounter with God. That day was his fresh start and the first day of his journey to the contented life in Jesus. In fact, Paul wouldn't even preach a message about Jesus for over a decade after the Damascan road. Paul, just like us, was on a journey to discover and rediscover who Jesus is, what He has done, and what that meant for his life. It would be close to three decades after his God encounter on the road before he ever wrote "I have learned in whatever situation I am to be content."

Paul's road to contentment was a journey and so is ours, which is why I could not pick a better model than Paul as we embark on this voyage.

My aim, my desire, my life goal is to learn to be content in whatever situation I may find myself in. If that's your goal as well, I invite you to journey alongside of me. I pray the pages of this book encourage your weary waiting soul, and help you learn how to live in every season, content.

––––––––––––

As we take this journey together over these pages, we want to be working from the same understanding. That's why we need to get clear on just what contentment is . . . and what it is not. Sometimes we think of contentment as that feeling that comes over us when all is right with the world, when all the circumstances and details line up just so. But that's not contentment. And it is not contentment because it is contingent on things outside of our control. Anytime I try to make my contentment dependent on other people's actions, reaching some goal I set for myself in ministry or fitness, or even just getting across town on time with no traffic, I'm confusing contentment with being soothed.

I have the most precious twin nephews. They are ridiculously cute, and I love my role as aunt to them, along with my other nieces and nephews. They were born a little early, so we all learned a lot of new things about working with babies who startle a bit more easily, have a little bit harder time digesting their milk, and who are also being raised in a home with adorable and noisy siblings. As I would rock and swaddle and burp each of those little babies, I would think about how content they would be once I got their diapers changed, got that feeding into them, got their siblings to settle down around them.

But here's the deal with those babies: That clean diaper I just got on one of them will get dirty. That bottle they drained will soon be a forgotten memory, and they'll be squalling for more. That "contented" nap they're taking in my arms (and, by the way, one million points to moms of twins! It's bananas, I tell you!), that nap will end, and we'll start the whole ordeal over again, diapers, bottles, and all. See, that kind of "contentment" is transitory and circumstantial, meaning that it doesn't last long, and it's all based on how those babies are feeling. I've successfully soothed them, but that's bound to change . . . and change quickly!

That's not the kind of contentment I'm talking about for you and me. I'm talking about the kind that sticks with you, even when the heartbreak comes. I'm talking about the kind of contentment that triumphs over an unhealthy restlessness. I'm talking about the kind of contentment you can stay in, you can rest in, even when things don't go the way you want or when life seems a little boring.

Or when life gets too dramatic.

That kind of contentment. It is not being soothed, although that has its place sometimes.

I want for you and me the kind of contentment that lasts.

Wanting What You Have, Not Having What You Want

I've heard it said: Contentment is wanting what you have, not having what you want. That sums it up well. It is embracing the life we have right now, the season we are in right now. It doesn't mean we don't have goals or vision, or that we don't aspire to be the best version of ourselves. It doesn't mean you put away those dreams you have.

It *does* mean that you don't put off living your life with joy and fullness, even when you are tempted to catalog what you think is missing. Contentment is a place of gratitude, a gratitude that sometimes confounds or seems at odds with specific details in your life.

And while we don't often think of it this way, contentment is power. Contentment protects you from the expectations and side-eye glances of those who think you should be at a particular place in your life by a certain age. Contentment frees you from the arbitrary timelines and deadlines we put on ourselves. Contentment gives you a magnifying glass to find joy no matter how small. Contentment is safety, a refuge from the disgruntled groans and jadedness of the world. Contentment is an antidote to fear. Contentment allows you not to take yourself too seriously. Contentment equips you to follow the contours of peace.

Contentment makes you at home, even when the circumstances of your life seem unfamiliar and strange.

Before we dive into the life and ministry of Paul, let's take a quick look at the words of James to see what robs us most often of living in a place of contentment. James was the younger brother of Jesus. Talk about pressure!

We don't know precisely when James got on board with Jesus's ministry. The book of John says it was not in the early days of Jesus's public ministry, "For not even his brothers believed in him" (John 7:5).[2] But at some point, James did become convinced that his older half brother Jesus really was the Messiah, and he spent the rest of his life teaching others about Him and pastoring a huge church in Jerusalem. The letter he wrote to the early church is full of practical advice and some pretty strong words about how to truly live in the grace we have received. He even addresses why we struggle to make contentment our home and instead resort to conflict with one another and with ourselves. "What causes fights and quarrels among you? *Don't they come from your desires that battle within you? You desire but do not have, so you kill.* You covet but you cannot have what you want" (James 4:1–2, emphasis added).[3]

Too often, where we live in our souls is a war zone. When a dream I've had gets smashed or something is taking a long, long time to come to fruition, my emotions start throwing bombs into the middle of my heart. You've been there, too. But a battleground isn't supposed to be our home.

Now, I get it. I understand that as believers in Jesus, we're going to do battle. Late in his life Paul tells his young mentee, Timothy, to "fight the good fight of the faith" (1 Timothy 6:12).[4] Paul elaborates this battle metaphor in his letter to the Ephesians when he says, "For our struggle is not against flesh and blood, but against the rulers, against the authorities, against the powers of this dark world and against the spiritual forces of evil in the heavenly realms" (Ephesians 6:12).[5] So, absolutely, we're going to have to fight in this life.

But we should be fighting against the dark forces in this world, not ourselves. When you and I allow discontentment to invade our hearts and to begin hurling its bombs of "not enough" and "when?" and "not fair" and all the rest, our protective borders have been breached, and we exist in that state James described so well, those "desires that battle within you."

Here's what I think: I think that Satan loves it when Christians are all up in their own heads. When we wring our hands over what we wish for that hasn't happened yet, when we live in a place of comparison and feeling like we come up short. When we put off living fully until sometime in the future, that whole "I'll be happy when . . . " phenomenon. I think he loves it because it keeps us so internally focused. And if he can keep us consumed with ourselves, then he keeps us living like babies, soothed by a fresh diaper, outraged by an empty bottle.

But we can grow up. Staying in a place of childlike wonder and faith, absolutely. But mature in our ability, through the power of the Holy Spirit, living free of Satan's schemes and aware of his tactics. One of Paul's highest aims was to help people get to a place of growth and maturity: "Him we proclaim, warning everyone and teaching everyone with all wisdom, that we may present everyone mature in Christ. For this I toil, struggling with all his energy that he powerfully works within me" (Colossians 1:28–29).[6]

But Paul was often frustrated by the discontent he found with believers when they acted more like they had colic than contentment. He wrote to believers in Corinth, "But for right now, friends, I'm completely frustrated by your unspiritual dealings with each other and with God. You're acting like infants in relation to Christ, capable of nothing much more than nursing at the breast. Well, then, I'll nurse you since you don't seem capable of anything more. As long as you grab for what makes you feel good or makes you look important, are you really much different from a babe at the breast, content only when everything's going your way?" (I Corinthians 3:1–3).[7] That last line of this passage gets me: As long as you grab for what makes you feel good or makes you look important, are you really much different from a babe at the breast, content only when everything's going your way? A discontented life will take us there every time, oblivious to how the enemy is whispering lies of comparison and jealousy to us, making us ever more fixated on ourselves.

So let's start with a true definition of contentment, that condition of our soul in which we trust, we live with joy, we stay in peace, regardless of what is swirling around us. And let's add to that understanding that contentment isn't just some pleasant state of mind: It's one of the very things that can keep us aware of and alert to the schemes of Satan. When we live in contentment, we wise up to how he will use comparison and envy to trip us up, how comparison leads us to making a bad relationship or financial or behavior decision.

Here's my challenge to you: Change your definition of contentment. And not just your academic definition, or one that you store in your mind and can repeat back to me by rote.

Think of it this way: A lot of us head to the gym, and we lift weights, and we start building muscle. And then once that muscle begins to grow, what's that word we start throwing around? Definition. We want our muscles to become defined. And for those muscles to become defined, it's not about trying to lift even heavier weight. It's about getting intentional about what we're feeding our bodies. It's about adding additional reps to the workout. And ultimately, when you're living in that place—where clean eating and consistent reps and the right balance of high intensity meet—then you start to see definition. There aren't any shortcuts.

That's where we want to get to over these next few chapters, where the muscle of our faith gradually takes on the definition of contentment, the place we live, the place that is home for us. It's going to take multiple reps of lifting our expectations and placing them in prayer before God with surrender. It's going to take multiple reps of lifting up our disappointments and allowing ourselves to be released from them. It's going to take a clean eating plan of consuming the word of God with intention. It's going to take cutting out the little extras, those cultural carbs we try to tag onto our understanding of contentment.

Contentment, when showing definition in our faith muscle, is the state in which we live, all the time, regardless of storm or sunshine. And if you are willing to adjust your understanding and make that kind of contentment your goal, well then, you're halfway there.

Contentment to the Core

I used to do a lot of running, and I loved it. But over time, I knew I needed to get stronger to my very core. So I adjusted how I was training. I set a goal to run a marathon before my thirtieth birthday. I trained for months. I also secretly hoped I would achieve a slimmer bod for my dreaded pending birthday. Instead of losing a few pounds, I actually gained weight. Due to all the calorie burning, I found myself needing to carb load . . . constantly. I craved mostly cheeseburgers, avocados, and fries. I needed strength training as much as endurance.

So I started lifting weights. I started doing planks. (Which I have a deep love/hate relationship with. Love what they do, hate doing them. That kind of complicated relationship.) I started doing burpees. And guess what? All the lifting and working for definition made me an even better runner. See, when we condition ourselves for strength and adaptability and definition to our very core, our ability to get even better in other areas expands.

Think about that. If you are willing to train yourself, with God's help, to get contentment settled deep into your heart, deep into your soul, embedded into your core, your spiritual race will become all the stronger. We have been trying to run the race of faith on the strength of our legs and our will only. But with contentment as central to how you live, then your whole being can move forward in more excellent balance, with greater strength, with greater intention.

Check out this amazing passage from Proverbs: "Do not let them out of your sight, keep them within your heart; for they are life to those who find them and health to one's *whole body*. Above all else, guard your heart, for everything you do flows from it" (Proverbs 4:21–23, emphasis added).[8]

What we're making our inner dialogue, how we are defining things for ourselves in the internal chatter we always have going—it affects everything. In fact, it affects our "whole body," Proverbs tells us. And when our definition of contentment doesn't match God's, it weakens us at our deepest level. It colors and hampers how we experience life. And when left unchecked, our flawed definition of contentment can make us heartsick to the core, when life batters against the shores of our sanitized dreams and blasts cold spray onto the fragile watercolors in which we paint our ideas of happiness.

So, yeah, how you define contentment, how I define it, it matters. We've got to start by getting it right if we're going to get well conditioned for exploring it in the following pages. Let's pinky swear (or affirm, depending on your theology), right here and now, that we're going to let go of searching for a contentment based on circumstances. Let's agree, right here and now, that we're going after a contentment that stands in spite of how we feel or what our circumstances may be. A contentment that cannot be taken from us. A home for the heart, built of contentment, that rests and trusts and believes that God has us, that He's for us. That we always have Him, no matter what shows up in our lives, is taken from our lives, never happens in our lives.

If contentment is wanting what you have, not having what you want, then let's get to the core of what we have: We have Jesus. And if we can start there, then we can learn the secret ways of contentment, we can embrace its mysteries, we can represent the calm in any storm because we know the One who calms the storm.

Let's get back home together, to a place called contentment.

Think About

Take a moment and read, ponder, and answer the following questions. As we proceed through this book, come back to your answers and see if they change or evolve by the time you finish this book.

- How have you been defining contentment?
- Have you considered contentment as something that comes and goes? What do you think about the idea that you can have consistent contentment, no matter what is going on?
- Do you associate contentment more with an emotion or with a decision?
- What makes it difficult for you to choose contentment?

Chapter 2

Content to Follow Jesus

One thing I can pride myself in is I'm pretty direction-ally keen. Put me in a new city one time, and when I return years later, I can manage my way throughout the city without much assistance needed. I inherited this trait from my dad. He calls it our internal GPS. I couldn't tell you which way is north, south, east, or west, but I'll get you to your destination, no problem.

After I graduated college, I got my first grown-up job working in the governor of Idaho's office. You know, the kind of job that has benefits and actually makes sense based on your college degree. Talk about feeling like a real adult all of a sudden. One of the major responsibilities of my job was travel-ing with the governor and first lady to speaking engagements and other events. Oftentimes I would be expected to pick them up . . . in my car. Up until that point, my parents had always had a car for me to drive (thanks, Mom and Dad!). At the time, I was driving my mom's black Volkswagen Beetle. I couldn't imagine picking up my state's most influential officials in my (well, my mom's) little two-door mini car. Especially since the governor was well over six feet tall. So I thought it was time to get my own grown-up car to match my grown-up job.

Hours later and after way too much money spent, I had bought myself my first car . . . fully loaded with a technology package that included a navigational system. Keep in mind, I lived in Boise, Idaho, the place where I had grown up and knew every single street by heart. So why in the world did I need to spend thousands of extra dollars for the tech package? Because I'm a sucker.

It didn't take long for me to realize that the fancy built-in navigation system in my car was completely unnecessary—at least until I moved to Los Angeles. Then I understood why these navigation systems were created.

Even though I'm good with directions and navigating through a town, I was not prepared for the largeness and stress of the L.A. traffic. Hence, that unnecessary, extravagant navigation system ended up coming in real handy. The only problem was that the GPS in my car only gave me turn-by-turn directions. I could only see one road at a time. I wasn't able to see the whole journey and understand how I was going to end up at my destination. I don't like not knowing how I'm going to get somewhere. I wanted the full picture of the journey, not just the next step. We typically want to know exactly how we are going to reach our destination.

Do you ever feel like that in life? I do, all the time. I love when God places promises in my heart, but what I would really love is to know exactly when and how I will reach those promises. Following Jesus is more like one turn at a time.

What's the most frustrating thing about following Jesus? Not knowing where the heck he is leading me. Anyone else? Jesus simply calls us to follow where He is going, not telling us where it will lead.

When Jesus calls the first disciples in Matthew's gospel, he doesn't lay out the map of their lives and tell them exactly where they are going and the exact way they will get there. I mean, not even a hint. All he says is, "Follow me."

> While walking by the Sea of Galilee, he saw two brothers, Simon (who is called Peter) and Andrew his brother, casting a net into the sea, for they were fishermen. And he said to them, "Follow me, and I will make you fishers of men." Immediately they left their nets and followed him. And going on from there he saw two other brothers, James the son of Zebedee and John his brother, in the boat with Zebedee their father, mending their nets, and he called them. Immediately they left the boat and their father and followed him. (Matthew 4:18–22)[1]

The disciples in this passage (Peter, Andrew, James, and John) did not know where they were going when they "immediately" started following Jesus. They had no clue where the road would lead them. Do you think Peter realized in that moment of deciding to follow Jesus that he would be considered the great foundation of the church one day (see Acts 2)? Do you think Andrew realized he would ultimately be revered in faraway places for the way he followed Jesus and served others? If you're wondering the answer, let me help you: NO! They didn't know where the journey would lead. All they could see was what Jesus was doing right then. They saw the miracles and signs and wonders. They saw people coming in blind and leaving with their sight. They saw lame people being carried in on their beds and then walking out carrying the bed. They saw the crowds of people, once broken, now whole. They saw God's kingdom invading earth, and they had to be a part of it! So they immediately started moving in the direction of Jesus.

You know what marks a follower of Jesus? Someone who hears God, obeys, and immediately starts moving in His direction. We've all heard the song "Reckless Love" by Cory Asbury. Every church, every church conference, and every youth camp in America has reminded us repeatedly that God's love is "overwhelming, never-ending, and reckless" for us. It's a great song, and God's love is absolutely all those things for us!

But "Reckless Love" only tells part of the story. I think there is more to God's love. God's love is so deep and wide for us; His love refuses to leave us where He finds us. Yes, God will chase you down. Yes, He will fight for you. But the moment you look God full in the face and acknowledge that reckless love for you—God will move you from that place He found you to a better place.

God loves us right where we are! Whether we're broken, lost, hurt, disappointed, and full of sin—He finds us right where we are. However, God loves us too much and refuses to leave us there. When He calls you to follow him, He's calling you to leave the place where He found you. You can't *follow* Jesus if you never *leave* where you're at. I think everyone is willing to accept God's love, but not everyone is willing to leave where they were found. Yes, God's love will chase you down, but he also keeps moving and invites you to follow where he is going. I wish they would add that part to the song.

So why is it so difficult for us to trust and follow where Jesus is leading us? Because you can't follow Jesus if something else is more important than Jesus.

Luke's gospel gives us a different picture of what we saw in Matthew and the real cost of following Jesus.

As they were going along the road, someone said to him, "I will follow you wherever you go." And Jesus said to him, "Foxes have holes, and birds of the air have nests, but the Son of Man has nowhere to lay his head." To another he said, "Follow me." But he said, "Lord, let me first go and bury my father." And Jesus said to him, "Leave the dead to bury their own dead. But as for you, go and proclaim the kingdom of God." Yet another said, "I will follow you, Lord, but let me first say farewell to those at my home." Jesus said to him, "No one who puts his hand to the plow and looks back is fit for the kingdom of God." (Luke 9:57–62)[2]

The difference between Matthew's text and what we see here in Luke is that the men in Luke's gospel needed the answers before they would choose to follow where Jesus was going. In other words, following Jesus was on their terms, not His. Jesus, Himself, wasn't enough for them. But Peter, Andrew, James, and John followed without hesitation.

The anonymous men of Luke 9 were more concerned with their comforts than they were about going where Jesus was going. To be fair, they probably had comfortable jobs, families, and lifestyles. That's a lot to ask someone to give up, isn't it? Well, Peter, Andrew, James, and John had all the same comforts, but they left those comforts to join the mission.

Let's look at this interesting segment from the above passage: "As they were going along the road, someone said to him, 'I will follow you wherever you go.' And Jesus said to him, 'Foxes have holes, and birds of the air have nests, but the Son of Man has nowhere to lay his head'" (Luke 9:58).[3]

What is Jesus talking about? Foxes? Holes? Birds and nests? Is this a zoology lesson from Jesus? Jesus knows that some won't be able to leave their comforts behind and follow where He will go. Practically speaking, Jesus and his disciples had to be okay with not knowing where they would sleep each night. He didn't have a travel itinerary with his hotel confirmation information for each town He entered. Where Jesus and his disciples slept, ate, and traveled was a journey of trust. And Jesus knew some wouldn't be able to trust enough and leave their comfortable beds behind.

Can we have a little real-talk moment? If we're honest with ourselves, the number-one reason we struggle to go where Jesus is leading us is that we value our comfort over Jesus. We don't want to sacrifice our comfort.

I love being comfortable, too! I love sleeping in my own bed instead of a mosquito net–covered bed in Africa. But I still go once a year to Kenya to teach pastors how to study and preach the New Testament in their churches. I like doing certain parts of ministry—like preaching, teaching, and training leaders—more than others. I don't love counseling sessions and one-on-one coffee appointments. But I do them because I value people, and people so desperately want to be heard and given encouragement and guidance. I love quiet nights at home alone where I can read by the fire or watch my favorite show without commentary from a crowd on my couch. But I open my house to create a community for people who might not have family to surround them. Now, this might not sound like a big deal to you, but the older I get, the more introverted I feel I have become. Let's not get crazy, I don't want to live in the mountains like a hermit, but I definitely want to be alone at home after a long day of being around people.

I think it's from all the pressure over the years of being a pastor and expected to be the life of the party. Now I want the party to be my pillow and me in bed by 10 p.m. I recently read about a hybrid personality, the ambivert. This personality adapts to their environment. In other words, an ambivert acts as an extrovert in social settings and an introvert when alone. This is 100 percent me. And when you're an ambivert pastor and always surrounded by people, it's a real sacrifice of your overall comfort to keep being around them. But to follow Jesus means that I sometimes need to leave the preferences of my personality behind.

The real problem with comfort is that it's intrinsically selfish. Being comfortable is all about what *I* want. And often we don't care if our comfort impacts anyone else. What if what makes me comfortable makes another person uncomfortable? What do we do then? You know this is why most cars have dual heating and air-conditioning systems now, right? Now the driver and passenger can each comfortably ride at their desired temperatures in the same vehicle. What did we even do before this witty invention? I'm pretty sure it has saved countless marriages.

———————

I have had to grow in the realization that my comfort is not more important than someone else's comfort. If turning on my ambivert switch one night isn't possible because some girls need some time hanging with their pastor, then my comfort is going to have to wait. This doesn't mean we neglect our own needs and refuse healthy self-care. But it does mean we can't obsess over our comforts more than the comforts of others.

Let's pick up another segment of the Luke 9 passage:

To another he said, "Follow me." But he said, "Lord, let me first go and bury my father." And Jesus said to him, "Leave the dead to bury their own dead. But as for you, go and proclaim the kingdom of God" (Luke 9:59–60).[4]

Jesus also had to correct His followers' view of traditions and what they believed was most important. Jesus is not saying "dishonor your parents" in this text. I've heard people read this scripture and then wrongly interpret that Jesus hates your parents and condones you dishonoring or being disrespectful to them. Bad hermeneutics, my friend. Neither the Bible nor Jesus will contradict themselves. Jesus believes and the Bible instructs you (see Ephesians 6:2) to honor your father and mother. Jesus is not saying, "Forget your family." In fact, recently, when I was studying and getting ready to preach, my mom was in a car accident. Her vehicle was T-boned, and her car was totaled. The police officer who was on the scene called me to inform me of the accident and to ask me to come get my mom. Did I say, "Well, Officer, I'm kind of busy right now getting ready to preach so I can tell people about Jesus. You know, the Lord's work, so I'm not going to be able to help my mom"? Of course I didn't say that. Instead, I jumped in my car, rushed to get my mom, spent three hours in the ER with her, and still made it in time to preach that night. What Jesus

is referring to in Luke 9 is human traditions that keep us from following Jesus, and burying your father was one of the traditions of the day.

The Apostle Paul dealt with this as he began planting churches. People followed traditions over Jesus. They followed certain church leaders over Jesus. It got to a point that Paul had to deal with it several times in the letters he wrote to the church. In his first letter to the church at Corinth, he had this to say: "I appeal to you, brothers and sisters, in the name of our Lord Jesus Christ, that all of you agree with one another in what you say and that there be no divisions among you, but that you be perfectly united in mind and thought. My brothers and sisters, some from Chloe's household have informed me that there are quarrels among you. What I mean is this: One of you says, 'I follow Paul'; another, 'I follow Apollos'; another, 'I follow Cephas'; still another, 'I follow Christ'" (I Corinthians 1:10–12).[5]

When we follow anyone over Jesus, whether that is a beloved preacher, or a way we feel comfortable doing things, or putting off following Jesus until we think things are a little more settled in our families, it means we can't follow Him fully. We're always following something. We've got to choose Jesus first if we are going to find contentment in Him.

The Jewish tradition of the day was that the oldest son's duty was to bury the father. The son was to wait and live near his father until he died in order to obtain the inheritance. Many Jewish families of the time regarded this obligation to

bury one's father as the most holy and sacred responsibility of a son, but Jesus is trying to indicate that this is secondary to the call to follow Him. Putting tradition, financial security, or the disciple's own desires over serving Jesus is the antithesis of following Jesus.

What traditions do we hold more important than following Jesus? We all carry so many traditions. The way we think and talk. The way we raise our children. The people we believe we are supposed to marry. The way we celebrate our holidays. The way we make green bean casserole at Thanksgiving. The way we "do" church. Traditions aren't bad. We all have them. But may I argue that many of our traditions start as opinions? We all have a lot of opinions, don't we? We have opinions about people, opinions about politics, opinions about social issues, opinions about raising kids, opinions about church, opinions about health and food. Opinions, opinions, opinions! And we hold on to these opinions very tightly. You would think our opinions had gone to a cross and saved us from our sins the way we defend and guard them. You don't believe me? Just go look through your Facebook newsfeed and tell me how many opinions are vehemently defended, and about the most ridiculous things.

The other day I saw a mom post on her Facebook page asking her friends their suggestions on how to relieve her child's severe eczema outbreak. You would have thought we were debating quantum physics given the passion and accusations that were being thrown. One mom started arguing with another over her "wrong" opinion about treatment, and then another mom started chiming in, dissing the first two moms. Before it was all over with, there was a whole chain of comments and insults and snarky remarks, everyone defending her position and no one ultimately helping the poor mom who had come seeking some information and insight. And not to mention the poor kid was still suffering from eczema. I'm not going to lie. I was quite entertained just watching from the cheap seats and not engaging, but I was also appalled at how dehumanizing our language becomes when someone else does not agree with our opinion. We have made opinions our savior over the One who actually saved us. Jesus' followers must guard against following opinions and traditions more than following Jesus. That's what Jesus meant by "let the dead bury the dead." If that tradition, if that opinion matters more to you than what Jesus is asking, then you've missed the point. Jesus supersedes all our traditions and opinions and gives us the way to live life.

And here's another way that we kid ourselves about following Jesus: "Yet another said, 'I will follow you, Lord, but let me first say farewell to those at my home.' Jesus said to him, 'No one who puts his hand to the plow and looks back is fit for the kingdom of God'" (Luke 9:61–62).[6]

This is classic human talk. "I will follow You . . . but first let me . . . ." We put all sorts of conditions on following Jesus. We condition it. We want church the way we like it. Not too short and not too long. We like worship at the right decibel while singing the right songs. We want our church to give more to missions in impoverished countries while demanding Disneyland-like classrooms and engaging mascots for our kids in the children's ministry department. We want God, but we want what we want more.

Fill in the blank: I'll follow Jesus when_____.

> I graduate from college.
> I get married.
> I have kids.
> My kids grow up.
> I become successful.
> I retire.

There will never be a more ideal time to follow Jesus than right now. Every season of your life will be busy. I remember thinking I was sooooo busy in college. Then I graduated and got that first real job, in the governor's office, and I couldn't believe people worked this hard and long every day. A lot of my friends are full on in the season of raising kids. They're driving them to school then basketball practice and friends' birthday parties and recitals and hopefully they will get their kid to church this week, but life is busy. Yeah, it's so busy that before you know it, your little kid will be all grown and still will have never made it to church because of your busyness, and then you will worry whether they will start following Jesus as they're away at college.

We have to fight the urge to place conditions on following Jesus. Following Jesus is right now. Today. In this moment. Not after the dance recital.

We have to be content to follow Jesus where He's going, how He asks us to get there, and when. Being content in following Jesus truly means that we trust Him more than we trust anything else.

Do you think Peter, Andrew, James, and John knew the pain they would endure as they embarked on this wild adventure of following Jesus? If they did, do you think they still would have said yes to the journey? They didn't know what we know now, that there would be generations of Christians who would be martyred before Christianity began to be accepted more broadly in the world. They didn't know what it might entail, but they followed, and they followed all the way to their own imprisonment and death.

Peter said yes to following Jesus and had no idea one day he would be persecuted for the gospel and crucified upside down in Rome. Andrew didn't know that one day he would be tortured and crucified on a tree. James didn't realize that his yes to Jesus would lead him to be beheaded by Herod. Thank God for John in this story; he died of old age. (Let's all claim John's testimony for our lives.)

None of these men knew what the journey would look like or where it would lead. They didn't decide to follow where

Jesus was leading out of fear, but out of trust. They didn't fear the future, and they didn't base decisions on fear. But I guarantee, even with their dying breath, they would have said that they would say yes to Jesus all over again, content in the knowledge that they had lived their best, most complete lives and would now head to their reward.

Just Enough Light for the Next Step

> *"Your word is a lamp to my feet and a light to my path."*
> —PSALM 119:105[7]

God's word is a lamp, but not a flood lamp. More like a flashlight. I imagine it more like the flashlight on my iPhone that helps me find my keys buried in the bottom of my purse, not necessarily a spotlight that beams far, far ahead on the road. God's word illuminates one step at a time because that's all we really need to see and know. Thank God He doesn't illuminate the entire journey. God simply lights up each step or turn when we need to see it. If we saw the whole journey from beginning to end, with all the twists and turns and ups and downs and trials and triumphs, and disappointments and joys—how many of us would ever say yes to Jesus? The good news about following Jesus is that we don't need to know where we're going. We just need to be near the one who knows where He's going, and that's Jesus.

One of my all-time favorite C. S. Lewis quotes says it best: "If you want to get warm you must stand near the fire: if you want to be wet you must get into the water. If you want joy, power, peace, eternal life, you must get close to, or even into, the thing that has them."

All we need is to get close to Jesus. You don't need an entire road map for your life. You just need the next turn illuminated. Jesus lights the way. Just stay close to Him. Be content to simply *be with Jesus*.

Jesus the Model for Paul

In order to identify counterfeit money, bankers are trained to study genuine currency. Bankers are not asked to spend hours staring at and examining counterfeit bills; rather they spend hours looking at the real thing. They can quickly spot a fake bill since they are certain what a real bill looks like.

Paul had that discerning eye. Jesus is the perfect archetype for contentment; Paul knew this better than anyone. Which is why Apostle Paul patterned his whole life after Jesus. That is what Paul gave his life to do, study the real, genuine, and authentic Savior who would show him the life of contentment. Which is probably why it was so easy for Paul to see what would lead him into discontentment . . . because, to Paul, it didn't look or sound like Jesus.

Throughout this book, we join Paul on his journey to study the life and way of Jesus so that we may know, with all certainty, what it means, looks like, and feels like to live in contentment.

Think About

- Do you feel like you are completely following Jesus right now? Or do you feel like you are holding back, even just a little bit? If you're holding back, what do you think is causing that? Is it an agenda you don't want to let go of? Is it fear of what it might cost you?
- If you were to follow Jesus fully right now, what would it cost you? What would you give up? Would it be a habit that you know is holding you back? Is it a relationship that is really fun, but often ends up being a bad influence on you? What step could you take, right now, to release that thing that's holding you back?
- Do you believe that following Jesus fully has the ability to lead you into contentment? Why or why not?

Chapter 3

Content in Christian Joy: A Version of Happiness

f I asked you "Where's your happy place?" or to "describe your perfect day," what would your answer be? Is your happy place on a beach somewhere listening to the ocean waves crashing against the shoreline, a little drink with an umbrella in your hand? Sitting around a dinner table with all your loved ones sharing a meal and laughing, with no conflict or drama? Is your happy place a sunset summer drive through the country with your windows rolled down, country music blasting on the radio, and the wind blowing through your hair, washing away your troubles?

We could all probably think of a happy moment or two. But that's the problem with happy moments. They're simply moments. And moments are fleeting. They're there one minute and gone the next. Eventually, you'll have to leave your drink with the umbrella in it and fly home to your real life, real job, real pressures. Next time you have a family dinner, maybe not all the family members make it a priority to attend, and the ones who do might be in a bad mood, not ready to enjoy the time together like you want. And there are only so many months you can drive through the countryside with the windows rolled down, enjoying the sights and smells of summer, before it becomes frigid cold and snowy (at least, that's true in Idaho).

My happy place is a very significant moment that happened a few summers ago. I had recently moved back to Idaho from the chaos of Los Angeles traffic, and it was right before my very favorite holiday, the Fourth of July.

I know, I know, most people would vote for Christmas or their birthday or Valentine's Day as their favorite holiday, but I've always had this massive crush on the Fourth of July, maybe because I was raised in Idaho, and the summers are glorious after the depths of winter, and the Fourth of July seems like a way to celebrate summer at its finest. Idaho summers are the most glorious thing ever. You can see sky for days, and it'll leave you breathless on a warm summer night where you just lay down and stargaze. But we pay for this, with interest, in our long winters.

This particular Fourth of July weekend seemed especially heaven-kissed. We started the festivities with an annual white-water rafting trip with some of my longest and dearest friends. As we were gliding down the glistening water of the South Fork of the Payette River, smooth times on the water punctuated by thrilling moments punching through the rapids, I looked up and saw a beautiful bald eagle soaring directly over us. A bald eagle? Our nation's bird? On the Fourth of July? Come on! Too perfect! I smiled as I soaked up the moment. Here I was living my best life.

A few hours later, we continued the Fourth of July extravaganza by heading to our church-owned campground, where we were camping as a family for the weekend. Our campground, Faith Heights in Donnelly, Idaho, is quite possibly my favorite place in the world. It's remote, tucked away from the noise of the city, and sits right on Cascade Lake overlooking a beautiful mountain range. The lake creates a polished blue mirror for all that big summer sky.

As we arrived at Faith Heights, the lake was in perfect condition for wake surfing, calm, glassy water just waiting to be surfed on. A group of us jumped on the boat to surf, and you would have thought Jesus Himself had come to calm the waters to perfect stillness. To top it off, the sunset sky was painted in colors I didn't even know existed. It took up the expanse of the entire sky and reminded me once again just how creative and carefully detailed God is.

As if the day wasn't already perfect enough, I ended this favorite holiday of mine by watching the best Fourth of July fireworks show of my life from the boat with my family. My whole heart, all my people, all in one boat together. That day, without a doubt, is my happy place. I captured pictures of that magical sunset that I'll never tire of seeing. It's now several years later, and it's still the wallpaper picture on my phone, a happy reminder of that happy place moment in time.

A year later, my glorious Fourth of July rolled around again. I had built up the last holiday so much in my mind and deep in my heart, and I had me some high expectations. But guess what? We hit some snags.

There was no bald eagle. No one wanted to go on the annual white-water raft trip that year. So instead, I headed straight to the campground, where the weather was uncharacteristically cool and windy for a Fourth of July in Idaho. The lake water was so choppy it looked like angry ocean surf; we would have looked like an episode of *Deadliest Catch* if we'd tried to go out in that wildness.

Finally, by late afternoon, the water had calmed down enough to take the boat out with the family to watch the fireworks show. Surely, I thought, surely, the day would be salvaged. The fireworks would make up for the less-than-stellar holiday. But even the fireworks were anticlimactic, to the point that no one knew the grand finale had happened. Which is awkward, I can tell you. Is it over? Do we clap? Do we keep sitting here?

The crowd slowly started to applaud after a long pause of no fireworks, until one more anemic remaining firework fizzled weakly in the sky. We sat there confused and wondered if there would be more, only to wait long enough to realize . . . nope, that was it. Not to mention, the mosquitoes were attacking us like crazy on the boat. And there is something deeply wrong with being chilled to the bone *and* getting bitten by mosquitoes. All the kids were crying and wanting to go to shore. Nothing about this Fourth of July felt like the last one. My happiness was gone.

On what had I built my expectations for that day? The last Fourth of July happiness.

Nothing seems more disappointing than unmet expectations . . . especially when they are related to what we think makes us happy.

If we're not careful, we can build our entire lives on the wrong version of happiness. And that happiness is almost always connected to what we believe to be "perfect conditions." The problem with this is that, as we all know, life is full of imperfect conditions. Life will have more imperfect moments than perfect ones. It's self-defeating to say, "When _____ [fill in the blank] happens, then I will be happy." I say self-defeating because you are setting yourself up for disappointment. You've spiked a ball above your head where the wind of life will catch it, and yet you're still expecting to be able to get the thing over the net. You've lost the game before you've even started.

Life rarely throws out consistent perfect conditions. Which is why Christian joy must look radically different from my version of happiness. If you build your life, like I did, on your one perfect day, then you'll never know what it means to live content every other day that's full of imperfect conditions. The degree to which you build your life around Christian joy is the degree to which you will find contentment in all circumstances.

If there's anyone who can teach us how to discover contentment no matter the circumstances, it's the Apostle Paul. Paul knows a thing or two about dealing with circumstances and overcoming them with joy like no one else. When Paul writes to his beloved friends in Philippi, he is sitting imprisoned in Rome. It's no secret that throughout Paul's life he suffered greatly. In fact, once he was beaten with rods in the very city, Philippi, that he now writes to encourage them to continue with joy and faith. At other times in Paul's life he was repeatedly whipped and also stoned and left for dead. And even our faith giant, Paul, at times found himself immensely discouraged in the midst of his hardships. One could even wonder if at times Paul felt depressed and defeated under such torture. He alludes to his deep discouragement in one particular passage in 2 Corinthians 1:8: "We do not want you to be uninformed, brothers and sisters, about the troubles we experienced in the province of Asia. We were under great pressure, far beyond our ability to endure, so that we despaired of life itself."[1]

"Despaired even of life?" Sounds like Paul is really losing hope here. And perhaps he did, temporarily. But that's what makes Paul such an incredible model of hope for us. As with all of us, Paul's hope can be temporarily lost, but he knew that a life with Jesus is never completely hopeless. Like Paul, we may feel like giving up, but also like Paul we can be sure that God hasn't given up on us. In the very next verse of 2 Corinthians 1, Paul lets us in on his secret to staying utterly hopeful in the face of wanting to give up: "Indeed, we felt that we had received the sentence of death. But that was to make us rely not on ourselves but on God who raises the dead" (2 Corinthians 1:9).[2]

Talk about contentment in the midst of circumstances. Paul wants the people of faith in Philippi to continue to rejoice in spite of whatever circumstance they might find themselves in. If he can do it, he knows the people of Philippi can do it as well.

In Philippians 4:4–13, Paul writes:

Rejoice in the Lord always; again I will say, rejoice. Let your reasonableness be known to everyone. The Lord is at hand; do not be anxious about anything, but in everything by prayer and supplication with thanksgiving let your requests be made known to God. And the peace of God, which surpasses all understanding, will guard your hearts and your minds in Christ Jesus.

Finally, brothers, whatever is true, whatever is honorable, whatever is just, whatever is pure, whatever is lovely, whatever is commendable, if there is any excellence, if there is anything worthy of praise, think about these things. What you have learned and received and heard and seen in me—practice these things, and the God of peace will be with you.

I rejoiced in the Lord greatly that now at length you have revived your concern for me. You were indeed concerned for me, but you had no opportunity. Not that I am speaking of being in need, for I have learned in whatever situation I am to be content. I know how to be brought low, and I know how to abound. In any and every circumstance, I have learned the secret of facing plenty and hunger, abundance and need. I can do all things through him who strengthens me."[3]

Paul used the noun *joy* and the verb *rejoice* twelve times in his letter to the Philippians, which is so powerful. Twelve times in four chapters is a lot! Joy, to Paul, is not momentary happiness. You're not experiencing joy if you're happy one moment and sad the next. Ice cream does not bring me joy; it may make me happy for a moment, but once that lactose kicks into my belly, I'm not feeling any joy. I'm "feeling" lots of other things (cramping, bloating, regret . . . oh the "joy" of lactose intolerance) but that happiness is long gone. Joy goes beyond circumstances or "the feels," as I like to call them.

Two Versions of Happiness: Happiness Versus Joy

Joy is not a feeling. Happiness is a feeling we experience when someone compliments us, or our significant other tenderly kisses us, or our kids all go to bed at the same time without needing fourteen bathroom breaks and eight glasses of water.

Joy is a choice. A choice when your spouse forgot to kiss you goodbye. A choice when your kids are all crying at the same synchronized time. Joy is a choice we can all learn to choose on the daily when we discover what Paul did. If we search for joy and happiness based on circumstances, we'll never find contentment or rest for our weary souls.

Have you ever tried to eat dessert after you're so full from a spectacular multicourse gourmet dinner? You don't want anything more to eat when you're full. Better than that—you don't need anything else. When you're full of joy, you have no room for discouragement, anxiety, fear, worry, resentment, or bitterness, because you're too full with something else—joy!

That's the point Paul was trying to make to his readers in Philippi. He knew they were scared. Scared for their lives. Persecution for the early Christians was a real, viable threat. They were fearful and anxious. Yet Paul reminded them to be full of joy even in the midst of the understandable fear. Joy and fear can't coexist. One will eventually overpower the other. And Paul hoped they would follow his lead and allow joy to overpower fear.

Paul learned (and modeled) how to be content with whatever was going on and wherever he happened to land, rather than looking for the right circumstances to make him happy.

"Rejoice in the Lord always," Paul writes; "again I will say, rejoice" (Philippians 4:4).[4] The word *rejoice* here in the original Greek language meant "be glad." Have you ever tried to be glad and sad at the same time? It doesn't really work, does it? When you're glad, you tend to be *full* of gladness, which means there is no more room for any other emotion. It's challenging to be discontent with anything if you're so full of joy.

———

Joy is what sets the Christian apart from the rest of the world. Anyone can be fine with fleeting moments of happiness, but it's Christian hope, which Paul models for us, that gives us a reason to find and live in joy no matter what. Pain has a way of showing us what really matters. It can be one of our greatest teachers or an unwanted friend, but necessary all the same. Without it, we would struggle to know what joy and happiness really are.

Like any normal human being, I grew up imagining a life full of happiness and of very little pain or discomfort. Seems logical and smart. Except that it's not very realistic.

There is a rising trend in our culture today to avoid pain and discomfort at all cost. We will go to great lengths to reduce "toxic" relationships and remove "triggering" elements from our lives. The problem with this theory is that in the process of throwing away toxic people or triggering circumstances we also limit our access to joy. How? Well, without the pain of death we cannot understand the joy of life. Without the discomfort of injustice, we can never understand the joy of freedom.

If trauma is what we spend our lives avoiding, then joy will be difficult to find.

When I wrote my last book, *Finding the Lost Art of Empathy*, it was my journey to allowing my pain and trauma to become joy. In 2007, I was convinced I had met the man I was going to marry. He was indeed a loving, caring, and kind man. Things I longed for in a future spouse. But the happily ever after we planned together quickly turned to tragedy when he took his own life.

Fourteen years later, I know the joy I experience now is a byproduct of the pain I had to embrace. And I won't pretend it was easy. I was angry, hurt, bitter, shameful, and confused. But I couldn't escape it. I wouldn't escape it. For even Jesus had to push through the pain to reach his intended destiny marked by joy. Jesus knew that the outcome of the cross was the answer to the evil in this world. So He set his eyes on the joy of freedom while enduring the pain.

Jesus is described this way in Hebrews 12:2: "looking to Jesus, the founder and perfecter of our faith, *who for the joy that was set before him endured the cross, despising the shame,* and is seated at the right hand of the throne of God" (emphasis added).[5]

A broken, messy, chaotic road always leads to joy. I had a choice in the midst of my pain to choose that long road to joy or the path of least resistance, to avoid the trauma or triggering thoughts so I could experience fleeting happiness whenever possible. I chose right.

Sometimes you have to give up your version of the story and accept God's. I certainly did. I had to give up my happily ever after picture and accept that God has a beautiful story written for each of us, but that story may have some twists and turns. We have to give up our version of what we think will make us happy and receive what God promises will give us everlasting joy.

We have to be honest and vulnerable and ask ourselves some tough questions. If my life doesn't turn out the way I hoped or had planned, is God still good? Yep. Is God still good, and does He still love you if you never get married? If you're never able to conceive as you've dreamt of your whole life? If you lose your job? If you lose your spouse? If you go bankrupt? If you get sick? If you lose a child? The way we answer these questions gives us a gauge for what we've built our lives on. We have to decide that the answer to all the questions is "Yes. God is still good." Is my life built on happiness that is fleeting and can be taken away? There can only be one perfect Fourth of July for me. And I'm going to enjoy every last ounce of those memories and soak them up, but that day will only ever be one special day at best. It can never be what brings me contentment for life.

Oftentimes, we have two different versions of what Christian joy is because we have wrongly assumed that bad things shouldn't happen to Christians. You cannot walk in complete contentment until you realize that it includes walking "in any and every circumstance," as Paul mentions in Philippians 4:12.[6] The tough reality for many is to face this truth: All the bad things that happen in this world can happen to Christians. We are not immune to suffering, pain, heartache, disappointment, trouble, hardship, sickness, danger, or death. Christians' circumstances are no different from others'. Bad things can and do happen to Christians. This is the reality of living in a broken world. A reality Paul understood.

But the great news is that no matter what bad things happen, God will take the bad and use it for good. Cancer, loss, disaster—those things will not become "good," but good can come out of difficulty and trial. Maybe not how we would prefer, or like, but there will be good that results.

This reminds me of another wonderful portion of Scripture written by Paul: "And we know that for those who love God all things work together for good, for those who are called according to his purpose" (Romans 8:28).[7]

We tend to want to make Romans 8:28 mean something that it doesn't. Paul is not saying in this letter to the Church in Rome that since your boyfriend broke up with you, God will now send a better boyfriend. Paul is not promising that all your dreams will come true; he promises you a *contented* life. You can lose all those things—the boyfriend, the dream job—and still have a joy greater than circumstances! Contentment is a joy that cannot fade or be taken away.

Why are Christians so frequently discouraged when difficulty comes our way? I think we have wrongly assumed that our faith in Jesus is our vaccine against the unexpected, the unwanted, the tragic, the confusing. We seem to think we get a free pass from these things since we love Jesus and go to church. Our joy will always be a roller coaster if we hold this wrong version of joy.

Everything that happens to you (good or bad) has the power to mature you and form you into someone who looks, sounds, thinks, and acts more like Jesus. God's goal is to make us happy and whole like Jesus. The most content person in human history, Jesus experienced no lack and had complete joy. No matter what you've done or what people have done to you, His joy can be full and complete in you.

Come to God. There is no joy or happiness apart from God. John 15:11 says, "These things I have spoken to you, that my joy may be in you, and that your joy may be full."[8] God desires that we would live with an overflowing abundance of joy, not fleeting happiness.

Our joy rests in being in Jesus. We have all that we need or will ever want because we are in Jesus. That is the secret to the joy Jesus had as He faced the cross. And it's the same secret to Paul's joy and contentment as he sat in prison. If Paul had been operating out of the way most Christians prefer to think about hard times and challenges, that there shouldn't be hard times and challenges in the Christian life, well then, he would have been in some deep mud.

But check this out. Luke, the physician who witnessed so many important events in the New Testament and who wrote such careful and detailed accounts, tells us about a time that Paul and his friend Silas were thrown in jail. We read about it in the sixteenth chapter of Acts. It wasn't the only time Paul sat in prison; he ended up in jail, under house arrest, and in Roman prisons several times throughout his work for the gospel.

He and Silas ended up in jail this time because they had driven a demon out of a slave girl. That sounds noble, but because that demon predicted the future through that slave girl, and because that had proven profitable to the girl's owners, the owners of that slave weren't all that thrilled with Paul and Silas's act of Christian kindness. They demanded the authorities get involved for what they saw as "lost goods." Paul and Silas were arrested, were stripped and beaten, and then they were shackled by their ankles in the stocks of the jail.

Around midnight that night, Luke records this intriguing detail about what Paul and Silas were doing: "Paul and Silas were praying and singing hymns to God, and the other prisoners were listening to them. Suddenly there was such a violent earthquake that the foundations of the prison were shaken. At once all the prison doors flew open, and everybody's chains came loose" (Acts 16:25–26).[9]

Okay, hold up a second. Paul and Silas were praying *and* singing at midnight? Stripped. Beaten. Flogged. Let's take that in. Stripped, beaten, whipped, backs bleeding, bruises tattooing their ribs. Not an Advil in sight. And they're in there, all propped up, having a little acoustic concert for the other prisoners when this earthquake hits.

A fleshly grasping for happiness can't understand that. A conditional kind of happiness can't generate that. It's something *other*, something more profound than those things we rely on to make us "feel good."

As the narrative unfolds, when the jailer came scrambling to the prison cell and realized all the chains were off the prisoners, and the prison doors were standing open, he got ready to take his own life. He knew his career was over. He had one job. Keep the prisoners in the prison. And he had failed to do that job. But Paul reassured him that all the prisoners were there and accounted for. Experiencing that kind of contentment with that kind of integrity changed everything for the jailer. In that moment, he wanted to know this Jesus about whom Paul and Silas had been singing. The jailer knew that he had encountered something that transcends anything else this life has to offer. Paul and Silas shared the gospel with him. He put his faith in God. The jailer took Paul and Silas to his home. He washed their wounds. And they, in turn, washed his entire family in the waters of baptism. Luke says this about the jailer: "He was *filled with joy* because he had come to believe in God—he and his whole family" (Acts 16:34, emphasis added).[10]

Now, remember, this was the guy who just a few hours earlier had been ready to take his own life because he was in such despair over the circumstances of that life. And yet now, with this encounter with these contented prisoners, who introduced him to a Savior of Contentment, he had found a life of joy that lasts. The story he'd been telling himself about this possible jailbreak and its subsequent consequences on his résumé and his life becomes an entirely different story when understood through a lens of joy.

That's what I'm talking about, friends. Can you sing even when your life circumstances feel like a prison? And can you sing loud enough to influence the very people you feel are holding you captive? That's a contagious joy. That is a joy that changes the world. Yours. Mine. And a jailer in a little town two thousand years ago.

Jesus, the Most Content of All

Jesus had a sincere devotion and joy for living out His Father's will. It's the same devotion and joy we can have in living out the will of God for our lives. Yes, I understand Jesus was the Son of God—which means He was both human and divine. But Jesus puts His humanity on display for us as He gets ready to go to the cross.

Even Jesus himself had a moment and wanted a better way, a different version, an alternative ending to the plan God had prepared for him. Right before Jesus would be arrested and later crucified, he found himself asking if God had gotten it right. Jesus was still fully human, and so imagine the very human emotions that would likely have been overwhelming Him at this moment. "And taking with him Peter and the two sons of Zebedee, he began to be sorrowful and troubled. Then he said to them, 'My soul is very sorrowful, even to death; remain here, and watch with me.' And going a little farther he fell on his face and prayed, saying, 'My Father, if it be possible, let this cup pass from me; nevertheless, not as I will, but as you will'" (Matthew 26:37–39).[11]

Jesus knew and understood the pain He was about to endure. In His body, He absorbed all evil, all sin, and all sickness for all humankind. To take on this sacrifice was not an easy task. It was not a painless task. Nonetheless, He took it on. Not His will. Not His preferred version. Not His definition. But His Father's.

You know what I have discovered in my life about joy and happiness? I find joy and happiness when I chase God's version. The same joy Jesus had in loving His Father and doing His will, which led him to the cross, is the Christian joy we can live in today (no matter life's circumstances). Let's not build our lives on a fleeting Fourth of July happiness. Let's build our lives on joy that is full and content, no matter what. Not my will, but His be done.

Think About

- What is one of your happiest memories? What about it makes it the happiest? Is it the location, the people, the occasion, the celebration?
- Given that this memory takes up some good space in your brain, how long was this actual event? Was it a few hours? A week?
- We don't remember every single event and moment of our lives, just a few that stand out. What does this tell you about trying to live always in a state of supreme memorable moments?
- Are there happy moments from your past by which you're now trying to evaluate every other moment? What does that do to your contentment? Does it throw you off course in choosing contentment?

Chapter 4

Content in Anxiety and Fear

don't handle stress very well. But does anyone, really? I shut down when life is crazy, and if someone asks me too many questions about my busy schedule I start to feel the room closing in on me. I escape, like everyone else, to Netflix, Instagram, and reality TV.

When I first started writing this book on contentment and studying the words of Pastor Paul, I thought the purpose would be to encourage people to fully embrace the season in which they find themselves. You know, like for singles to enjoy being single, for young parents to embrace the chaos of raising children, for the empty nesters to find purpose in a new and different life. It didn't take long for me to realize that this was a very surface analysis, and represented only one minimal part of contentment.

What about being content when you feel overwhelmed by anxiety and fear? Where is contentment in that?

Cue a season in my life that has included anxiety and fear.

It was shortly after my thirty-eighth birthday. I found myself sitting in the room of another doctor's office, tired of feeling overwhelmed, not being able to sleep, and being extremely anxious. But not the panic attack kind of anxiety that I'd once had, but the everyday, all-day sense that life was out of my control. I had found myself in doctors' offices a lot that year, trying to figure out the mysterious symptoms that continued to haunt my body. We did extensive blood work and examinations, medications were prescribed, and then other medications, trying to fix what was starting to feel unfixable. Nothing was working.

So there I was hoping a different doctor would have a different remedy to fix me. As the doctor asked probing questions about my health history, he typed thorough notes from our conversation, with occasional "uh-huhs" as he rapidly typed. After what felt like the entirety of the hour-long appointment, he looked up and said, "I think we need to treat your PTSD. [post-traumatic stress disorder]."

PTSD? My first thought was: I've never been to war. Isn't that what our brave soldiers get from fighting for our freedom oversees? My second thought was getting the heck out of there.

But as the doctor explained his recommended therapy, I realized I had some un-dealt-with trauma.

Here I was thirty-eight with no husband and no children. Which, culturally, feels like a death sentence. In much of the Christian culture women's value comes from being someone's wife or someone's mother, and I was neither. And without my realizing it, the tragic death of my would-be husband over a decade earlier had traumatized me in a lasting way. I would push men away even though I desperately wanted them to love and choose me. I seemed to be able to attract a man, but I couldn't keep him. And I felt stuck and overwhelmed by anxiety.

I started feeling so much anxiety I would feel sick almost all day long. Then I would worry about how sick I was feeling, so I would naturally look up my symptoms on WebMD and self-diagnosis myself with whatever disease WebMD told me I might have. Within a few weeks, I had diagnosed myself with two different cancers and three autoimmune diseases. That's finally how I found myself in the doctor's office that day.

What I then knew was that I had grieved the death of my past, but I hadn't healed from the traumatic experience. Because healing trauma means you have to go back to the pain. And what crazy person would ever go back to what hurt them?

Hit of Dopamine

Anxiety disorders in the United States are considered the most common mental illness, with over 40 million sufferers in the U.S. alone. That doesn't even include the millions more who experience a low-grade degree of anxiety from time to time. Which would probably include all of us.

There is no question that anxiety is a major issue in the United States today. But why? Why do so many people suffer from anxiety?

According to a *Psychology Today* article, recent studies continue to show that "higher amounts of screen time are associated with higher levels of anxiety and depression." While some may escape anxiety through their screen, the time there might cause more anxiety, especially if you start comparing your life to the picture-perfect lives of the people you follow on social media.

So, why do we continue to scroll through, post, and wait for likes?

I know social media gets a bad rap, but it kind of deserves it. With all the benefits, advancement, and global connectivity that social media brings, it also has a shadow side. Which is best described by Facebook's first president, Sean Parker, in an article in the *Guardian*: "He explained that when Facebook was being developed the objective was: 'How do we consume as much of your time and conscious attention as possible?' It was this mindset that led to the creation of features such as the 'like' button that would give users 'a little dopamine hit' to encourage them to upload more content."[1]

The feeling of getting "likes" on social media has been likened to the same dopamine release one gets from taking drugs.

As described in *Business Insider*: "When someone likes an Instagram post, or any content that you share, it's a little bit like taking a drug. As far as your brain is concerned, it's a very similar experience. Now the reason why is because it's not guaranteed that you're going to get likes on your posts. And it's the unpredictability of that process that makes it so addictive. If you knew that every time you posted something you'd get 100 likes, it would become boring really fast."[2]

Trust me, I've been there. Lonely Friday nights when I saw everyone else and their dog out on a date or having a family movie night. And I was home by myself feeling alone, isolated, and unloved. So you better believe I found the best picture, the most inspiring quote or scripture, to get my hit of dopamine.

The problem is if someone does not get this "hit of dopamine" (in other words, doesn't get likes), they are increasingly being found to feel isolated, alone, anxious, and without peace.

Parental Peace

There are two types of people in this world: parents and non-parents. I am not a parent yet, but I basically feel like a full-time observer of parents since I have a front-row seat to my siblings raising their kids. One of the most outstanding observations I've made is my siblings' unbelievable ability to *not* hear their children's screams, repeated requests ("Mom, Mom, Mom, Mom, Mom, Mom"), or constant fighting. It's seriously like white noise to them.

A few years ago I took a road trip with my sister Rachelle, my brother-in-law Mark, and their girls, Kenzington and Chloe, who were ten and three years old at the time. We were headed up to the mountains for my favorite holiday of all time, which, as you know by now, is the Fourth of July. As we were leaving the house, Chloe grabbed a harmonica that was sitting on the kitchen counter. As soon as we had all settled into our seats for the two-hour drive up the windy road, the Chlo Chlo (as I affectionately call her) pulled the stolen harmonica out of her pocket and began to serenade the car ride.

The good thing about a harmonica is that just about anyone can sound good playing one. The bad thing about a harmonica is the person playing it determines just how loud the sound is and how often a high-pitched note is hit. And let me tell you, Chloe sure liked to hit that high note often and loudly. At first, it was pretty darn cute listening to this little three-year-old composing her own song. Twenty minutes into it, however, in the back, Kenzie—who was trying to watch a show with headphones on her mobile device—found her little sister's musical composition not so impressive. Kenzie couldn't take it anymore and started yelling at Chloe to stop playing, which, as you probably know, only causes a three-year-old to play louder and longer. Which only causes a ten-year-old to get more and more frustrated.

All the while, my sister and brother-in-law were somehow oblivious to the chaos in the rows behind them. But since I was in the back, too, I couldn't escape the ruckus. At one point, I thought about opening the door and rolling out of the car. That sounded more peaceful than what I was experiencing inside the car. Too far?

Parents are incredible. They can somehow live in a tranquil state of peace amid the chaos of their children. It truly is an *unexplainable peace*. The Apostle Paul describes a similar, but far better, unexplainable peace in his letter to the Christians of Philippi. Let's read again that passage from earlier, but let's read it in a slightly different translation this time, just to get a fuller flavor of what Paul is saying:

> Rejoice in the Lord always. I will say it again: Rejoice!
> Let your gentleness be evident to all. The Lord is near.
> Do not be anxious about anything, but in every sit-
> uation, by prayer and petition, with thanksgiving,
> present your requests to God. And the peace of God,
> which transcends all understanding, will guard your
> hearts and your minds in Christ Jesus. (Philippians
> 4:4–7)[3]

Remember, Paul is writing in a Roman prison to the Christians in Philippi. The Christian existence in a pagan world was full of uncertainties and anxieties: Persecution of one kind or another was always a possibility for these early Christians. Christians were worried about being persecuted for their faith, which was not an irrational fear. I mean, their great apostle, who led many of them to Jesus, was currently sitting in prison for preaching the gospel. Unlike most of our fears, this was a reality many were actually facing. These early Christians had likely seen friends and family burned at the stake in Rome, or at least imprisoned. Yet Apostle Paul speaks of peace in the midst of this anxiety.

The peace of God does not mean the absence of conflict or even unfortunate circumstances; it means the presence of Jesus during the chaos. Peace is not even the absence of anxiety. The peace of God is the reality of God's presence in the midst of the anxiety.

Peace That Will Guard

"And the peace of God, which surpasses all understanding, will guard your hearts and your minds in Christ Jesus."

The Greek phrase here, translated as "will guard," was a military term that meant "garrison (protect, guard, keep)." A garrison would likely have been quite familiar to the readers of the day, because of Roman rule throughout the region.

Paul declared that God's peace stands on duty like a garrison calming our anxious hearts. Just imagine that picture of a body of soldiers standing between you and your anxiety. That is precisely what Paul described. So why be anxious?

The peace of God does not mean the absence of conflict or anxiety. The peace of God exists in the very midst of chaos or anxiety. God's peace goes beyond our human understanding because we cannot understand how we could experience so much peace in the very heat of battle. God's peace surpasses how we think. Our thoughts are full of anxiety, but God's thoughts are infinitely higher than that.

When we pray to God, whose ways and thoughts are higher than ours, then peace has access to fill our hearts and minds. His peace transcends our anxiety. That's the gift we get when we go to God in prayer. Peace can flow out of our prayers and petitions to God because we don't have to know everything . . . God does.

How do you get the peace of God? Well, Philippians 4:9 tells us . . . by getting the God of peace.

"What you have learned and received and heard and seen in me—*practice these things, and the God of peace will be with you*" (Philippians 4:9, emphasis added).

Get to know God, and you will have His peace, even when chaos is swirling around you. You can't have the peace of God without the God of peace—they go together!

Right before Jesus goes to endure the most gruesome death in human history, He leaves us with this: "Peace I leave with you; my peace I give to you. Not as the world gives do I give to you. Let not your hearts be troubled, neither let them be afraid" (John 14:27).[4]

God does not submit to anxiety. Anxiety must submit to the peace of God. You can live content in God's peace, even when anxiety is spinning around you. Remember, it's Jesus who has the final word on your life, and that word is peace. Nothing shows the world Jesus quite like peace in an anxiety-driven world. I think I've demonstrated Jesus more in the seasons of my life where my world felt like it was drowning in anxiety, yet I chose to practice prayer and let God's peace stand as garrison between me and anxiety. You don't need your circumstances to change to feel peace. You need to practice praying to God, and you will see the God of peace rushing in to stand between you and the anxiety that tries to overwhelm you.

Remember, peace is not the absence of conflict. So if you're waiting for all the friction in your life to dissolve before you can be content in God's peace, you'll be waiting a long time.

Imagine this. You're driving your car along in the heat of traffic, and as you approach a light, you notice it's green. But instead of going, you're just going to wait for all the cars and chaos to pass you before you go. That's insanity! But it's often how we treat God's peace in our lives. He has given us full access to it, but if we're going to wait till the dust settles, until the chaos dies down, until our circumstances change, until we feel better, then we'll just continue sitting at the green light.

No.

The peace is there.

Access it.

Avoid Triggers

I used to think I could get rid of my anxiety and fears by pretending they didn't exist. Anyone else try that? Yep, doesn't work.

I'm a panicker. My mind goes to a dark place fast. When my mom doesn't answer my text within 4.3 seconds or if her phone goes straight to voicemail, if I'm not careful, I can immediately start sifting through all the possible terrible scenarios that could have taken place. She was walking to the mailbox and got mauled by a bear. She left her phone at home, her car broke down, and now she is stranded and has no way of contacting anyone. Wow, that escalated quickly. Calm down, Trace.

Some time ago, no one considered trauma to be a kind of nonphysical pain. Now we've grown accustomed to the diagnosis PTSD as an emotional as well as physical experience. Many young people today will quite automatically speak of their PTSD from child abuse, sexual abuse, loss of loved ones, or even betrayal by family or friends. For many of them, the defense they've developed is to spend the rest of their lives avoiding "triggers" to memories of that trauma.

The other day I saw a girl post on Facebook, "TRIGGER WARNING." Without realizing it, we have become a people who think avoiding the triggers to our pain, discomfort, frustration, and fear will free us from the anxiety the pain caused us. When in reality, we can only become free from the fear and anxiety of our pain when we let Jesus meet us in it.

I have recognized that fear can so easily exaggerate what's really happening. And many of us hold and carry irrational fears throughout our lives.

Every once in a while when I have to get up and use the restroom in the middle of the night, when it's cold and dark, I think back to a show I watched as a kid where there was a snake in the toilet, and then I immediately think my fear is warning me about something in the here and now. I become so fearful to use the restroom, even though I know that fear is irrational.

Many of us have more faith in our fears than we have faith in God. I've been there. Like, all the time. It truly is the "good fight of faith" for me every single day.

Too many times, we think, If only this bad circumstance would change, then I would be happy and content and free of all anxiety and fear. But have you ever had a "bad" situation change, and found yourself still not happy or still anxious? That's because contentment is not based on any external circumstance or situation. It's based on the goodness and largeness of who God is. We can trust His character. And His character is good. God can't be anything other than good. So we can rest and be content knowing that God is working out the details of our lives in spite of our circumstances.

After the doctor told me I needed treatment for PTSD, I immediately tried to hold back tears. For twelve years I had been holding on to pain that I wouldn't let anyone see, even Jesus. The doctor explained how the therapy would work. Essentially, the goal of the treatment is to emotionally go back to the place of pain and slowly cause the traumatic memories to fade. I was extremely skeptical, but also desperate. I quickly found the moment and memory that I most needed healing from. It was amazing how I let myself go back to the very moment I never wanted to be at again. But this time, I brought my brokenness and I brought Jesus into the pain so he could heal it. My doctor told me at the end of the session that he had never seen anyone release something so quickly and with only one session. That's how desperate I was to be free.

The Bible says, "There is no fear in love, but perfect love casts out fear. For fear has to do with punishment, and whoever fears has not been perfected in love" (1 John 4:18).[5]

The way we find freedom from fear is not by ignoring it but by embracing something bigger than it is, like love. The moment you identify the fear and replace it with something more substantial and better, like God's love, fear can't rule you. You have to get vulnerable with your weaknesses and concerns so that you can be content in God's love.

Thoughts Are Powerful

On my thirty-eighth birthday, while I was traveling and speaking in Australia, I discovered a rash on the trunk of my body. I've rarely had rashes in my life, so I certainly thought it was strange, but nothing to freak out about—until I returned home to the U.S. When I came back, the rash had gotten worse, so I went to an urgent care center. I was immediately told I had shingles. Shingles? Telling a single girl who just turned thirty-eight that she had shingles was like kicking a horse when it was down.

A few days later I made an appointment with my primary care physician just to make sure the urgent care doctor got it right. Dr. Karl has easily known me most of my life. He means a lot to our family and has always been an exceptional doctor. It was Dr. Karl who discovered and had to give the news to my then seventeen-year-old brother that his life would be dramatically altered with a type 1 diabetes diagnosis. Dr. Karl knows our family history and knows us all personally quite well, and he always makes me feel better by the time the appointment ends.

This particular time was no different. As Dr. Karl opened the door to the exam room in which I was waiting, he smiled, and I smiled back. I think we were both smiling because, like I mentioned earlier, I've been to the doctor more in the past year than I went in the past several years. So I can only imagine what Dr. Karl thought when he saw me . . . *again*.

He looked at me and said, "What's going on?"

With a little giggle, I replied, "I have shingles." He looked at the rash and confirmed what the previous doctor had told me at urgent care, that it was indeed shingles.

He asked how I was feeling overall, and I told him I felt fine. But in the two days since I had been initially diagnosed with shingles, I had become Magnum P.I. on the internet to discover what symptoms to expect with the disease. And boy, did I think I felt them all. I told Dr. Karl I was good, but that I felt tingling all over my body. As I waited for him to respond with some sympathy or sadness for my pain and plight, he looked at me straight in the face and said, "No, you don't."

"What? Yes, I do. I feel some tingling in my leg and my hand right now!" I exclaimed.

"No, you don't," he answered again. "The mind is a powerful thing. You think you feel that, but you don't."

Dr. Karl went on to explain scientifically and medically what my body would be experiencing. And it wasn't the tingling all over my body like I had convinced myself.

And, oh my word, was he right! The moment I left his office, I never felt those phantom tingles again. You might think he was being insensitive or wasn't listening, but remember, he knows me. And he knew my thoughts were running wild with all things shingles. The brain is a mighty thing. Our thoughts are powerful things.

Have you ever thought about something so long, you began to believe it was true? Our minds have the power to dwell on things that are true or false. Paul helps us to think about what we're thinking about.

Here in verses eight and nine of Philippians, Paul shows us how to frame our thoughts:

Finally, brothers, whatever is true, whatever is honorable, whatever is just, whatever is pure, whatever is lovely, whatever is commendable, if there is any excellence, if there is anything worthy of praise, think about these things [or "dwell on these things," in the NASB translation[6]].

What you have learned and received and heard and seen in me—practice these things, and the God of peace will be with you. (Philippians 4:8–9)[7]

Paul believed that something else should occupy our minds rather than anxiety and fear. He understood the influence of one's thoughts on one's life. To Paul, right thinking always leads to right living, while wrong thinking will always lead to wrong living. Paul borrowed the practice from secular writers of his day and listed essential virtues that should occupy the mind, saying *we must* "think on these things."

The verb translated as "think on these things" means a lot more than simply "keep in mind" or "think about." It likely means something deeper, for instance to "take [them] into account" and reflect carefully upon so that they can shape your life.

We need self-evaluation of our thoughts. We could indeed be in the deepest, darkest place of our life, and pretending the thoughts aren't there will not help us walk in freedom. We have to take account of our thoughts. Your mind might be dark with low thoughts about yourself. Take account. So, you can reframe and reshape your life. Your mind might be a constant stream of negative thoughts. You have to stop and evaluate them.

The worst thing we can believe is that things will go away on their own. The sad reality is that if we don't think about what we're thinking about and reframe our thoughts, then the shape of our life will not be contentment.

Change Your Brain

Pardon me while I nerd out just a little. Neuroplasticity is one of the greatest scientific discoveries to have been made in recent years. Neuroplasticity means our brains are malleable and can be reshaped based on our thinking patterns. Cognitive neuroscientist Dr. Caroline Leaf says in her book *Think, Learn, Succeed,* "You can change your brain with your mind, and, by doing so, change your life."[8] Our thoughts are potent in improving our lives, from our health to lowering stress, to feeling more joy. The mind is a powerful thing to waste, they say. "A thought is not only a thing,"[9] says scientist and author Lynne McTaggart, "a thought is a thing that influences."[10]

Neuroplasticity is great news for someone like me! I have all the power to change my thoughts, which will, in turn, change my life! Too many Christians spend so much energy focusing on behavior modification. I don't know about you, but the more I try to stop a bad behavior, the less success I have. However, the moment I start to think about where that pattern of behavior stems from in my mind and how I can think differently about it, then I'm able to deal with the thoughts and thought patterns, and eventually, the right behavior follows.

Take account of your thoughts. Self-evaluate what you spend the majority of your time thinking about. Dr. Leaf says, "What do you think about the most? Whatever you think about the most will grow; if you are thinking about something daily, within approximately two months, your brain has changed to accommodate this pattern of thought. Whatever we think about the most will have the most energy and will dominate our thinking, the good and the bad."[11]

Most of what we need starts with what we believe! And what we believe begins with thoughts. As a pastor, I've learned that one of the biggest challenges in helping people overcome addictions and struggles is to get them to understand that the first place to help overcome the power of addiction and struggle is in the mind. Our brains are influenced and shaped throughout our lives by what we allow them to think, meditate on, and believe. I'm the college and young adult pastor at my church, and most of my job is to get young adults to think higher thoughts of God. It takes practice when for most of your life you have been focusing on negative thoughts about yourself and your relationship with God.

Perhaps you were sexually abused as a child by a male authority figure. Most of your life, your thoughts toward that abuser and likely other male figures have dominated your beliefs about what men in general are like, how father figures are, and have thus been projected (subconsciously) onto how you believe Father God must be, too.

Imagine your brain has all these neural pathways connecting to different responses. If you were abused as a child, you feel angry and full of shame. If you hear the abuser's name or see him (or her), that fires a series of neurons together. The first time you think "I hate him, I'm so angry," you've created a pathway in your brain. As you keep having the same negative response, you strengthen that negative neural pathway.

Before you know it, it has become such a natural pathway that it doesn't even seem abnormal to be always angry and full of shame. The response is so familiar and comfortable to you that you have formed a habit. It started in a completely understandable way, because of the horrific abuse you suffered, but it can go on to dominate your thoughts and ultimately your life, making the abuse even more costly to you.

Our brains are so powerful and so malleable, they will adapt and even change to whatever our responses are, which is fantastic news! If you're anything like me—someone who has built some pretty intense negative neural pathways—you can change them!

Scientists agree that we strengthen whichever neural pathways we use the most. Which is where we get the old saying "Neurons that fire together, wire together." We can create a new pathway in our thoughts, which will shape our brains, which will lead to right behavior. It just requires practice!

I see Paul as one of the original neuroscientists. He told us what science is trying to say to us today: Your thoughts will translate into action, so make sure your thoughts align with these virtues, because your actions and life will then reflect them.

He started the list of virtues with whatever is true. True is what is real. Anxiety creeps in as an intruder to our lives when false ideas occupy our minds instead of truth. We have to settle our minds on the truth; otherwise, we will find ourselves with anxious thoughts that lead to anxious behavior. When we don't rest in what is true and real, we'll settle for fantasy.

Now, no offense to any of you who love *The Bachelor* or *The Real Housewives*. But we often look for places of escape, and for many it's reality TV, or fantasy books and movies like *The Hunger Games* or the Twilight series. The moment I let my heart drift from the truth of who God is, it's easy for me to escape to another world altogether. It seems to me that one reason people love reality TV is because they don't want to face the truth of their lives and thoughts. When life gets hard. When our thoughts overwhelm us. When we feel overcome by anxiety. When we feel pushed into a corner, our kneejerk reaction is to escape to something not real (even if it is called "reality" TV). We can hide in fiction. We don't have to deal with stuff in fantasy. We can brush everything under the rug and hope it disappears by the time we decide to reenter the real world. Fantasy, and heightened reality, is an escape from actual reality, from the *truth*. We have to be willing to expose our true thoughts and bring them out of hiding.

We live in the age of "know your own truth." I don't want to know my own truth! My truth sucks! My truth gets me in trouble. My truth wants me to late-night online shop for retail therapy and buy things I don't need. My truth makes me live by feelings and causes me to make colossal mistakes in relationships. I don't need my truth. I need God's truth!

The cultural milieu and context today are that there is no absolute truth, so we better fend for ourselves and not screw up too badly. This is so far from what it means to live as a Christian.

It's this kind of rhetoric that causes many Christians to fall into fantasy so they can escape the truth of God's reality. The reality is that God's truth is the only *truth*. So we must learn to live by that instead of our experiences, finite understanding, and philosophies (because they change). But God never changes!

Thinking on the truth is thinking on Jesus, who is the truth. He said it Himself. "I am the way, and the truth, and the life. No one comes to the Father except through me" (John 14:6).[12] The way we start building strong and healthy neural pathways is by knowing the truth! Truth is our starting point.

Do the Frameworks

Practice framing your thoughts. Your thoughts need a frame to help keep them contained and in perspective. Think of a frame as the search history on your internet browser. Have you ever Googled something and then it always seems to pop up later? Maybe you have been online shopping for that perfect winter boot, and now every time you go to search something on the internet—boots pop up! Those boots have become the frame around your searching. It's similar to how our thoughts get framed.

I love this story that Eugene Peterson, pastor, writer, and thought leader, tells about visiting a member of his congregation who was struggling with her thought life, and the insight she had about what she needed:

As I entered a home to make a pastoral visit, the person I came to see was . . . embroidering a piece of cloth held taut on an oval hoop. She said, "Pastor, while waiting for you to come I realized what's wrong with me—I don't have a frame. My feelings, my thoughts, my activities—everything is loose and sloppy. There is no border to my life. . . . I need a frame for my life like this one I have for my embroidery."[13]

How do we get a framework for our anxious, worried, and negative thoughts? How do we reframe our negative neural pathways to become positive neural pathways? How do we get the right thoughts that will lead to right living? We let our thoughts about God become more frequent than our thoughts of fear, inadequacy, concern, worry, and anxiety.

Just like the search engine that caught on to my searching algorithm for boots, so our brains catch on to our daily thoughts about God. The more you "search" (think) about God, the more your thoughts will be framed by God.

You need to frame your thoughts around God's infinite wisdom and unmatched power. Whenever I can tell my thoughts and life are starting to feel sideways, I almost inevitably and immediately begin reading the book of Psalms, that beautiful collection of writings by King David and several other writers. There is just something about the poets' words and descriptive language of an almighty God that settles my anxious thoughts. Remember, anxiety is an intruder that often creeps in when we start to believe a lie about God, rather than the truth.

We might start to think:

God doesn't care about me.
I'm never going to feel better.
I'll never have the life I thought God promised me.
God has forgotten me.

When we start to fill our minds with these lies, the first thing we must do is replace them with the truth. And there's no better place to replace a lie about God with the truth than in the reading of the word. Let this one fill you with truth!

Even the darkness is not dark to you;
   the night is bright as the day,
   or darkness is as light with you.

For you formed my inward parts;
   you knitted me together in my mother's womb.
   I praise you, for I am fearfully and wonderfully made.
   Wonderful are your works;
   my soul knows it very well. (Psalm 139:12–14)[14]

Wonderful are His works, and He has perfectly formed me! Now that's truth I can frame my life on!

Think About

- Have you experienced that peace of God before, the kind that transcends whatever was going on in your life? What was it like?

- How is "peace" different from "calm"? Do you sometimes confuse the two?

- Have you struggled with anxiety? How does it play out for you? Does it make you sick physically? Does it drive you to behaviors that are unhealthy for you, but are how you've coped?

- Have you used prayer as a last-ditch effort in the past when it has come to managing the worry, fear, and anxiety that sometimes come upon us? What do you think might change if you made prayer the first thing you ran to?

Chapter 5

Content in Suffering and Shame

Suffering is a part of our story. Yet it's the part of our story that many of us as Christians struggle to embrace. Or we simply want to deny its existence. Our Christian relationship to suffering is similar to how the world views cancer. We know it exists, but we assume it won't happen to us.

Paul was no stranger to suffering, and he had an unbelievable ability to power through hardship that came his way. Paul was not ignorant or naïve about the human reality of suffering in this world. In fact, from the beginning of Paul's ministry, after he preached the gospel in different regions and planted churches there, he immediately started preparing those new Christians for suffering.

> After they had proclaimed the good news in that city and made many disciples, they returned to Lystra, to Iconium, and to Antioch. They strengthened the souls of the disciples and encouraged them to continue in the faith, saying, *"We must enter the kingdom of God*

through many persecutions." (Acts 14:21–22, emphasis added)[1]

So it should not come as a complete shock to us when Paul "boasts" about his sufferings. He had long prepared for them:

Five times I received at the hands of the Jews the forty lashes less one. Three times I was beaten with rods. Once I was stoned. Three times I was shipwrecked; a night and a day I was adrift at sea; on frequent journeys, in danger from rivers, danger from robbers, danger from my own people, danger from Gentiles, danger in the city, danger in the wilderness, danger at sea, danger from false brothers; in toil and hardship, through many a sleepless night, in hunger and thirst, often without food, in cold and exposure. And, apart from other things, there is the daily pressure on me of my anxiety for all the churches. Who is weak, and I am not weak? Who is made to fall, and I am not indignant? If I must boast, I will boast of the things that show my weakness. (2 Corinthians 11:24–30)[2]

"If I must boast, I will boast of the things that show my weakness." This was a radical statement in Paul's day. He was going against the very fabric of the Greco-Roman and Jewish cultures' definition of shame and failure. The cultural milieu of the day was to boast about your achievements. The sufferings

that Paul boasts of are the very antithesis of human achievements and honor to the world. Not unlike today, no one in Corinth at this time was sharing their weaknesses, failures, and humiliating moments.

We understand this. Cue Instagram filters that magically take away every sun spot and wrinkle, every dark circle under our eyes. We want to look like a million bucks! We would rather die than show the world of Instagram how we really look when we wake up in the morning. Why? Because the fallen human condition craves the admiration of others. Remember the social media dopamine hits we talked about earlier? We want to showcase our achievements, because achievements get the attention of others, and we have carried this into our understanding of God—so we believe that it is our achievements that also get us the attention of God.

Paul knew that it wasn't human achievements that demonstrate the grace and goodness of God. Rather, grace and goodness are demonstrated in our weaknesses. Yes, even through suffering. God's grace being demonstrated through weak things is what the whole Christian story is about. Without God's strength being demonstrated through His son on the cross, we would have no Christian narrative to discuss today.

Paul understood this better than anyone. Which is why he writes, "If I must boast, I will boast of the things that show my weakness."

He goes on to say, "For the sake of Christ, then, I am *content* with weaknesses, insults, hardships, persecutions, and calamities. For when I am weak, then I am strong" (2 Corinthians 12:10, emphasis added).[3]

Can you say you are content in your weaknesses? Can you say you are content in the suffering you may have endured? Paul could and did. Paul was not some superhuman Captain America that we can never live up to. Paul was a broken man, saved by the grace of God, who let his life be a parade of God's grace to the world.

That's what suffering does. It actually puts God's love and grace on display. But we have to have a correct understanding of God's love.

The great Christian thinker C. S. Lewis sought to reconcile the great debate between the goodness and power of God with the reality of evil and suffering. Lewis called this "the problem of pain."

"If God is good and all-powerful, why does he allow his creatures to suffer pain?" Lewis writes in his book *The Problem of Pain*.[4] Great question! And one we would all probably like the answer to.

"Try to exclude the possibility of suffering which the order of nature and the existence of free wills involve, and you will find that you have excluded life itself."[5] This is often our short answer to getting rid of the problem of evil. If God is so good and omnipotent, then he should just eliminate evil and suffering altogether, right? The only problem with this solution is that it provides another problem. If you get rid of evil, you also must eliminate free will. C. S. Lewis's rebuttal to this might be "the freedom of a creature must mean freedom to choose: and choice implies the existence of things to choose between."[6]

Ultimately, we as Christians struggle to accept suffering. We don't think we should suffer. The question of theodicy is the biggest question in the human heart. Why do bad things happen to good people? And why does a good God allow it? There has never been a simple answer to these questions. We may never know why accidents happen, or how parts of our DNA make mistakes that lead to diseases, or why our spouse defaults on our covenantal commitment through adultery.

What we do know is that Jesus suffered not just like us but also for us. What we forget is that on the very first Easter Jesus defeated evil. Evil is contained and will one day be completely eliminated. But we must remember that the Christian story is not over yet. One day there will be no more suffering, tears, sadness, sickness, or pain. One day there will be God's justice flowing like rivers. But until that day, God's love remains so that before the fateful day we will choose Him.

We must embrace God's way. We may never understand suffering, but we can embrace God's love in spite of our suffering.

Once again C. S. Lewis says it better than I ever could: "What would really satisfy us would be a God who said of anything we happened to like doing, 'What does it matter so long as they are contented?'"[7] Lewis goes on to say that what we really want is not a father in Heaven but a grandfather in Heaven whose sole purpose is to see "young people enjoying themselves" and that ultimately "a good time was had by all."[8]

Maybe it's not suffering we should spend our lives avoiding. Perhaps it is the right definition of God's love that we should seek.

Name the Shame

I think a lot of contentment in life is robbed by shame from our suffering. Even if we are able to "boast in our weaknesses" like Paul, the collateral damage of shame still haunts our ability to live content. So many of us relive our past pain or mistakes, but we don't want anyone to know. We may think and dwell on it, but we would never speak of it. I battled with a lot of shame for many years after I told the man I thought I was going to marry yes on a Friday, and then he tragically took his life on the following Tuesday. For years, I carried the shame of thinking I wasn't enough for him, wasn't enough to make him want to stay in this life. The shame of rejection. The guilt of feeling worthless and unlovable. The shame of not recognizing the pain he must have been in, the despair in him. I would never express these things to people, but I certainly felt them every day.

The shame from my past pain caused me to feel alone and unable to find contentment.

But something about the woman with the issue of blood in Luke's Gospel really resonated in my spirit. Let's read her story:

Now when Jesus returned, the crowd welcomed him, for they were all waiting for him. And there came a man named Jairus, who was a ruler of the synagogue. And falling at Jesus' feet, he implored him to come to his house, for he had an only daughter, about twelve years of age, and she was dying.

As Jesus went, the people pressed around him. And there was a woman who had had a discharge of blood for twelve years, and though she had spent all her living on physicians, she could not be healed by anyone. She came up behind him and touched the fringe of his garment, and immediately her discharge of blood ceased. And Jesus said, "Who was it that touched me?" When all denied it, Peter said, "Master, the crowds surround you and are pressing in on you!" But Jesus said, "Someone touched me, for I perceive that power has gone out from me." And when the woman saw that she was not hidden, she came trembling, and falling down before him declared in the presence of all the people why she had touched him, and how she had been immediately healed. And he said to her, "Daughter, your faith has made you well; go in peace."

While he was still speaking, someone from the ruler's house came and said, "Your daughter is dead; do not trouble the Teacher anymore." But Jesus on hearing this answered him, "Do not fear; only believe, and she will be well." And when he came to the house, he allowed no one to enter with him, except Peter and John and James, and the father and mother of the child.

And all were weeping and mourning for her, but he said, "Do not weep, for she is not dead but sleeping." And they laughed at him, knowing that she was dead. But taking her by the hand he called, saying, "Child, arise." And her spirit returned, and she got up at once. And he directed that something should be given her to eat. And her parents were amazed, but he charged them to tell no one what had happened. (Luke 8:40–56)[9]

"The woman with issue of blood," as she's referred to in the book of Luke, had spent every last penny she had on doctors' bills to find a cure for her affliction . . . but to no avail. Her disorder, this continuous flow of blood, made her ceremonially unclean, according to Leviticus chapter fifteen. Anyone or anything she touched would also be considered unclean according to the law. If she accidentally bumped into someone at the marketplace . . . that person was now also unclean. Which means this poor woman had lived twelve long and painful years in solitude and loneliness.

"The woman with the issue of blood" is the only way she is described in the synoptic gospels. (The synoptic gospels are Matthew, Mark, and Luke.) Thus, she was entirely defined by her problem.

In the ancient world, a woman who was bleeding for twelve years would have been considered permanently unclean, meaning she likely was not married, and would not be able to marry. Even if she had been married before her blood condition appeared, her husband would have likely divorced her. She was alone. She was isolated from the public. She was quarantined for twelve years from her family. And had no place in the community. If she went out in public, to the market or somewhere, she was supposed to shout "Unclean! Unclean!" to warn the people around her so they would not accidentally touch her and become unclean themselves. By law, she could be stoned to death if she accidentally touched someone and caused them to be unclean.

When we meet this woman in Luke 8, she was probably at the end of herself. She had gone to every doctor she could find and spent all her money and still was not healed. She likely had no friends. No community. No support.

Can you imagine the shame?

Can you imagine the loneliness?

Let's reread these verses and notice what the woman's shame caused her to do:

And there was a woman who had had a discharge of blood for twelve years, and though she had spent all her living on physicians, she could not be healed by anyone. *She came up behind him* and touched the fringe of his garment, and immediately her discharge of blood ceased. And Jesus said, "Who was it that touched me?" (emphasis added)

The desperate woman with no more hope fought through the crowd to get to Jesus. Her desperation caused her to go out in public—people were probably accidentally bumping one another, pushing one another trying to get close to Jesus. But her faith in Jesus caused her to push through the crowd. She should have been shouting "Unclean! Unclean!" to let the people know that she was present. She had to know she was doing something wrong by being in public this way, but she was desperate for Jesus's healing touch.

But still, her shame caused her to come up behind Jesus and touch Him. Isn't that just like shame, to make you feel unworthy to approach Jesus or even look Him in the face? Her shame kept her in hiding, and instead of approaching Jesus and looking him in the face she felt she had to sneak behind him, hoping not to be noticed. After all, if the crowd knew what she had done by elbowing and pushing her way to see Jesus, they could stone her.

We have to remember the context of the text. Context gives us the details, the circumstances, around a situation so that we can more fully understand what is going on. The context in this situation is that Jesus was on his way to Jairus's house to heal Jairus's daughter. Jairus was a big deal. The ancient world was built on hierarchy, and Jairus, as a leader in the synagogue, would have been at the top of that hierarchical ladder.

But when it comes to Jesus, and His ability to sense shame and need, we can't rush too fast to the story of Jairus. Nope. First, Jesus has an unscheduled encounter with this woman:

And Jesus said, "Who was it that touched me?" When all denied it, Peter said, "Master, the crowds surround you and are pressing in on you!" But Jesus said, "Someone touched me, for I perceive that power has gone out from me."

Jesus interrupts His own mission to call the woman out of her shame and hiding. Unlike everyone else in the past twelve years, Jesus addressed the woman directly, freeing her from her prison of shame. Jesus delayed his mission to heal Jairus's daughter. In fact, that delay initially costs Jairus's daughter her life. (Don't worry. Jesus raises her from the dead.) Freeing someone from their shame means that much to God.

The Psychology of Solitary Confinement

Solitary confinement is thought to be the worst psychological torture you can cause a human to suffer. Often it happens in a bathroom-size cell with fluorescent lights where one is left alone for twenty-three hours a day, with maybe one hour of exercise but no social interaction. The mind and identity decay if left too long in solitary confinement.

I recently finished watching a docu series about Ted Kaczynski, the "Unabomber." I was a young teenager during the time Ted Kaczynski was arrested for his domestic terrorist acts of mailing bombs and killing three people and severely injuring dozens more. What was fascinating about the docu series was how much the pain of Kaczynski's past seemingly motivated his rage and anger, but also his shame. Kaczynski was found living in a very remote area of Montana, in a cabin he'd built, with no running water or electricity. He had very little contact with the outside world. He had isolated himself from his family and his once successful vocation as a mathematics professor at UC Berkeley. His cabin wasn't much larger than the solitary jail cell he would later be in for the remainder of his life.

Pain and shame motivated Kaczynski to shut out community and escape from society. We certainly don't go to the extremes of the Unabomber, but we do shut out community and avoid relationships when we feel full of shame.

Shame Motivates Us to Hide and Withdraw

After we have experienced an embarrassing and hurtful breakup, we stop wanting to go out with our friends, or we have a difficult time being vulnerable with a new potential love interest. We're afraid they might discover what the last person disliked and run away. So it's easier to hide and binge-watch Netflix and not think about it.

Perhaps we feel the shame from a bad investment or a business venture gone wrong, and thus we refuse to take a risk again, and instead we hide from any future great opportunity. We would rather play it safe than get burned again. So we live in a self-imposed solitary confinement. Like the woman from Luke's gospel.

Jesus's love and compassion for this woman motivated Him to call her out of hiding. He did not call her out to embarrass or shame her in any way. He called her out of hiding and made her name the shame, the thing that was holding her back, the thing that was her burden, not to embarrass her, but to free her!

There is freedom in being able to tell and laugh about your most humiliating moment. You feel released from the humiliation, once you can put voice to it. That's essentially what Jesus asked the woman with the issue of blood to do.

Name it!

"And when the woman saw that she was not hidden, she came trembling, and falling down before him *declared in the presence of all the people why she had touched him*, and how she had been immediately healed" (emphasis added).

She had to face the people who often ridiculed her, and tell them she had walked into the crowd unclean. She had to admit that she probably touched them while she was pushing her way to Jesus. She had to look at them in the face, not knowing what they would do to her. Jesus was tenderly drawing her out of hiding by making her affliction and healing public.

Jesus knew the only way to free her was to make her shame known. And as soon as she did, her full healing came.

Then the most unexpected and spectacular thing happened.

Jesus didn't call her by her shame or her issue ("woman with the issue of blood"); He called her by her true identity . . . daughter! Check this out! "And he said to her, 'Daughter, your faith has made you well; go in peace.'"

The woman who was unclean for twelve years, who probably hadn't been touched or hugged or called by a name other than "the woman with the issue of blood," was now called "daughter."

Jesus called her out of hiding so the entire crowd would know that this woman was now healed and free from her shame. She was now clean! She could be restored to full community and society! It was the end of her physical affliction and also the end of an unbearable loneliness. If Jesus hadn't called her out, she would have gone right back to her prison of shame, and no one would have known she was whole.

Shame will try and tell you who you aren't, but it makes you believe it's who you are. Jesus comes to call you by your true identity—a full, whole member of the family.

Shame makes you feel like an outsider. Jesus makes you whole.

We can't walk into contentment if we're still bound by shame. Contentment can't find its home in shame. We have to be willing to name our shame and let Jesus rush in and make us whole the moment we are honest.

Jesus doesn't heal what we conceal. We're only as free as we are honest!

Get honest with God. He already knows what shame we carry, but he also knows that contentment is available on the other side of our willingness to name the shame that has kept us shackled.

His love has never changed.

For us, we need to realize that what hinders our spiritual growth is often not the need for more information, more sermons, more podcasts, more worship music, more prayers. All those things are good. But what really hinders us is our unwillingness to be honest. Honesty with ourselves, with others, and with God throws off the confines and allows our spiritual growth to blossom and flourish.

Once we are honest about the things we have hidden, then we can experience the complete transformation available from the gospel we already know. The irony is that our shame and pain is not hidden from God. He already knows, but He stops in the path of our lives so that He can call us out of hiding.

I believe the greatest miracle of this story in Luke is not that the woman was healed, but that Jesus made her whole! Jesus also wants to make you whole.

Friend, Jesus doesn't just want to heal you. He wants to make you complete. Why? Because He has a plan for your life and a plan for you to lead others to the total freedom you found in Jesus. But if you don't let God heal you from your shame and pain, the only place you can lead people back to is your solitary confinement. Fragmented lives full of shame, pain, and guilt can never show people freedom and wholeness. Only whole people can do that.

Have faith like the woman with the issue of blood. Fight through the crowd to get close to Jesus and let Him heal you, but don't let him just heal you; let Him free you from your shame.

I told you earlier that I carried overwhelming shame for years after the tragic death of Tennyson, the man I thought I was going to marry. When I finally named my shame to Jesus, God so tenderly gave me this promise that I hold so close to my heart, and I want to share it with you if you're struggling to give God the shame you have been carrying.

> *Instead of your shame there shall be a double portion*;
>> instead of dishonor they shall rejoice in their lot;
>> therefore in their land they shall possess a double
>>> portion;
>> they shall have everlasting joy. (Isaiah 61:7, emphasis
>>> added)[10]

God wants to give you double for your trouble! That sounds like a good deal to me. Give God your shame and let Him bring you double blessing and everlasting joy!

Get Bigger Thoughts

Am I the only one who sees a backpack left unattended at an airport and then is certain it is a bomb? It's not entirely my fault. I was a freshman in college when the attacks of September 11, 2001, gripped our nation. In fact, I will never forget that morning watching the planes hit the Twin Towers in New York City live on television. The worst part for me was when the news announced that a plane was headed for the U.S. Capitol, which my parents were two blocks away from. My sister and I frantically tried calling both our parents' cell phones and the landline of the house where they lived part-time in Washington, D.C. All the lines gave a busy signal. For hours we were unable to get ahold of our parents, who eventually contacted us telling us they were safe and were inviting congressional staff members, who were running down the streets screaming and crying, to come in and pray.

So, I grew up with the "see something, say something" generation, and I assume evil and danger lurk everywhere. Being cautious is great! Using wisdom and discernment is even better! But what isn't great about this catchy phrase is that it taught me to trust my feelings over everything. It's often why Christians start looking for the devil under every rock. Because something feels or seems wrong. There will likely be times when our feelings are correct and something is wrong, but there will be a lot of other times when our feelings are dead wrong. The more you "feel" something, the more it becomes true to you, whether it is or isn't in actuality true.

This is why we need to get bigger thoughts! Dr. Rick Hanson, in his book *Hardwiring Happiness: The New Brain Science of Contentment, Calm, and Confidence*, tells us, "Your brain is the most important organ in your body. What happens in it will determine what you think, feel, say, and do." He goes on to say, "The brain is the organ that learns, so it is designed to be changed by your experiences. . . . Whatever we repeatedly sense and feel and want and think is slowly but surely sculpting neural structure."[11] We talked about this a little earlier when discussing neuroplasticity, and I think it bears repeating: Your brain truly is the control center of your body. Yet we spend little to no time focused on this most important organ. We spend time taking care of our heart, our liver, our kidneys, etc., but we forget to check in with our brain, which is actually the organ that ultimately impacts all the rest of our organs.

Because the brain is an organ that learns, it is designed to be changed by habits and experiences (positive or negative). The way you change your brain is by changing your mind and thoughts. Whatever you focus your mind on will shape your brain.

So: Your experiences matter. Your thoughts matter. What you pay attention to—what you rest your mind on—is the primary shaper of your brain.

If bad experiences dominate your mind and thoughts, then that's what will shape your whole being, because your brain is the control center of your body. No wonder Paul says in Colossians 3:2, "Set your mind on things above, not on things that are on earth."[12] In other words, set your mind on bigger things, not on bad experiences, bad decisions, bad moments!

Think of it this way. Negative thoughts are intruders. They have no right to your mind unless you give them access. Can you imagine if I saw a guy walking up to rob my house and, to make it easier for him, I just swung the door open and said, "Come on in, sir. Take whatever you would like." You would say I was insane! Well, unfortunately, that's often what we do with our thoughts. We swing wide the door to our thoughts and allow just anything to walk in.

So how do you get rid of an intruder? If a robber came to your house, the way you would get rid of him is by getting something bigger and stronger than the intruder. You have to intimidate the intruder. I'm pretty sure an alarm system going off, the police showing up, or a weapon in the robber's face would intimidate that intruder.

Or think of thoughts of shame like a bully. There was a bully when I was in eighth grade. He was a foot taller than all of us, had a full beard, and had flunked so many times he should have been a sophomore in high school by then. Instead, he was stuck at Lowell Scott Middle School, and he terrified us. Every day after school, he would rush to the bus lineup and wait to scare and beat kids up. Every day, when the last school bell run, fear would rise up in our little eighth-grade hearts because we never knew if we were going to be the kid he tried to beat up. I remember one kid (probably the smallest among us) said, "Let's all lock arms and run to the bus at the same time." Power in numbers. I liked it. I felt safer knowing we were all going together. So everyone from bus 83 locked arms and ran as fast as we could to the bus so the bully couldn't get any of us. And sure enough, we were too big for him to handle.

The only way a bully will back down is when someone bigger and stronger than the bully shows up. That's how you get rid of bullying thoughts! You get bigger thoughts to replace them.

> For my thoughts are not your thoughts,
>> neither are your ways my ways, declares the Lord.
> For as the heavens are higher than the earth,
>> so are my ways higher than your ways
>> and my thoughts than your thoughts. (Isaiah 55:8–9)[13]

Think About

- What's our weapon? What's more powerful than an intruder? God's word. When you get God's word in your mind, it starts to overwhelm the intruder thoughts that try to discourage and derail you. Get bigger thoughts!
- Where your thoughts go . . . your life goes, so, get big thoughts. Your life will feel full and abundant, as well!
- What shame do you need to name?
- What kind of power has this shame had over you?
- How would it feel to be free of shame, by naming it and casting it onto the capable shoulders of Jesus?
- Why have you held back from naming this shame?
- Are you ready? Are you prepared to exchange your shame for contentment?

Chapter 6

Content to Risk over Safety

've already told you how much I love to wake surf. It's probably my favorite thing in the world. But a few years ago, I had an opportunity to learn to really surf. In the ocean. With sharks.

When I was pastoring in Los Angeles, I got to know the coolest girls in the world—surfer girls! I mean, can we just all agree that girls who can surf the ocean are just naturally cooler than the rest of us girls? Two particularly great surfer girls I know are Kelia and Bruna. And not only did Kelia and Bruna both surf, they happened to be professional surfers. When they invited me to Hawaii one weekend to watch a surf competition and spend some time with them, it didn't take me very long to agree.

While the girls were busy doing work for their sponsors, Kelia's mom, Tammy, asked if I wanted to learn to surf at her surf school right on the beach, so of course I said yes! I had wanted to learn for years. Plus, how perfect to learn from someone who actually teaches surfing for a living. Tammy taught me the fundamentals: how to paddle, how to jump up and position my weight and body, and how to look for a good wave. Tammy said I'd caught on quickly to the technique, and so we began catching baby waves (you know, the ones super-close to shore . . . where literal babies are playing in the surf, too). I was nailing those waves and feeling pretty good about myself.

After a while of me catching the small waves and learning the rhythm and technique of surfing, Tammy turned to me and said, "You're doing so great. Let's go out further now." The "further" that she pointed to was *far*. Far enough where it seemed like a shark or two might be hiding out looking for a bite to eat. And it seemed more advanced than I was ready for in my day one of surf lessons, but I trusted Tammy to know my skill level.

So off we went to the big waves. First of all, no one warned me that just paddling out that far would sap all my energy. No wonder you see surfers just lounging around, shooting the breeze in the middle of the ocean. They're winded. They've gotta catch their breath before they can catch a wave.

By the time Tammy and I got to the spot she had previously pointed out, I was winded from paddling. I listened intently to every single word, syllable, and fluctuation so I would know exactly what to do. Tammy calmly reminded me of all the things I had already learned and put into practice at the baby waves—she assured me that all the same techniques I used with the baby waves I would use with the bigger waves, too. She kept telling me how easily I had picked it up, which was building the confidence that I needed. For a few moments, we just rested on our surfboards, chatting. Tammy would see a wave coming, but she would explain why we wanted to hold off and wait for a better one.

All the while, I was listening and hoping a shark was not going to emerge from the deep blue at any moment and take me down with him. I was finally starting to relax as the waves and water calmed me. I remembered how good I'd done on those baby waves. My self-talk was confident . . . borderline cocky at this point. One of these bigger waves was just a couple of baby waves stacked on top of each other; I could do this, no problem.

Then Tammy shouted, "Paddle, paddle, paddle, paddle!" Without hesitation, I started paddling as fast as my little arms could go. I felt the push of the ocean's power moving me up and forward. I did what no one should ever do: I turned my head to look behind me, and in a moment, all my confidence vanished as I saw a massive set of waves tumbling right toward me.

The waves crashed against me. Not once. Not twice. But multiple times the waves kept pulling me under the water. I wasn't strong enough to get out of it, so I submitted to the wave until eventually the crest had passed and I surfaced.

Coughing, maybe crying, but undoubtedly terrified, I looked at Tammy and said, "I'm good." We finished our surfing lesson and paddled back to shore.

You might think I regretted ever learning to surf after that terrifying experience of going under the water. In that moment, I had forgotten everything I had learned and wanted safety over risk. But guess what? It was worth the risk. Because now I can say, "Yeah, I surf," and I did something that pushed me further than I'd thought I was capable of. If you had told me before I started my lesson with Tammy that I would paddle out in front of such a big wave, I wouldn't have believed you! But there I was, paddling as hard as I could. And what would have happened if I hadn't looked back, if I hadn't gotten scared and doubted myself? Maybe, just maybe, I could have gotten up on my board and ridden that colossal wave. Contentment will not always mean safe. It will take risk. But the risk for contentment is always worth it.

Safetyism

Remember how risky we were as kids? Growing up in Idaho, where we have some of the best white water in the world, I took a white-water rafting trip every year. People come from all over the world to see the rushing white water of our Idaho rivers because of the rapids' high levels of difficulty. Rapids are generally classified under six categories. A class one rapid is classified as moving water with small waves. If you're just trying to relax and get some sun, then a class one rapid is your speed. Class two rapids are still pretty easy and only require minimal paddling by rafters. Class three rapids are when things start to get exciting. This is when the rapids start to reach four feet in height and require more paddle participation from rafters. But its class four and five rapids that really get your heart pumping. These rapids are long, narrow, and difficult to maneuver. This is when you really see where the white water got its name. Class six rapids are the most extreme the river offers and should only be attempted by expert kayakers.

As a kid, I couldn't wait for our annual white-water raft trip. I lived for weeks in anticipation of the adrenaline-inducing, heart-pumping, thrill-of-all-thrills adventure—class five rapids.

One year we experienced several class four and five rapids on our river trip. One of the guys in our raft was a forty-something river virgin from California. He was petrified the entire trip. As we approached one of the class five rapids, our river guide yelled, "Everyone paddle!" Whenever the river guide yells and asks everyone to paddle, you know something crazy is about to happen and you better just paddle. The rookie rafter, who happened to be sitting in front of me, lost all control of his paddle as the raft rocked and spun, and he knocked my little twelve-year-old self right into the raging white water. Luckily one of the other rafters saw what happened and grabbed my hand and held me through the terrifying rushing water. Besides some bruised and bloody legs . . . I was great! Couldn't believe what a thrill I had survived and couldn't wait to do it again.

When did we stop wanting to take the risk? Was it at a certain age that we started valuing safety over risk? Was it in the way our parents raised us? Was it what the world inevitably taught us? I can't pinpoint the moment, but it happened. I get scared right before we go rafting now. My mind races with every possible scenario that could possibly go wrong; I wonder why on earth I'm putting myself through this.

Scott Bader-Saye, in his book *Following Jesus in a Culture of Fear*, talks about the new Christian ethic of safety:

> Fear tempts us to make safety and self-preservation our highest goals, and when we do so our moral focus becomes the protection of our lives and health. Security becomes the new idol before whom all other gods must bow. In the past, when asked "What is your chief goal?" Christians have given answers such as "friendship with God" (Thomas Aquinas) or "to glorify God and enjoy him forever" (Westminster Catechism, seventeenth century). Today, I suspect many Christians would echo the culture in naming "safety" or "security" as the primary good they seek.[1]

Don't get me wrong; safety is good. An important virtue to hold. But virtues carried to extremes can quickly become vices. The shadow side of overvaluing safety is that it can lead to the absence of our traditional Christian virtues of love, peace, and generosity.

Much of society today has changed what safety even means. Safety, until our modern era, meant physical safety. Safety now has drifted into a subjective definition. We now define safety as physical and emotional. So anything you decide that makes you feel "unsafe" is deemed so. In the book

The Coddling of the American Mind: How Good Intentions and Bad Ideas Are Setting Up a Generation for Failure, authors Greg Lukianoff and Jonathan Haidt describe this overvaluing of safety, which they call "safetyism": " 'Safety' trumps everything else, no matter how unlikely or trivial the potential danger."[2]

The value of risk versus safety has never been a more dominating dinner table conversation than it is now. With the risk of contracting Covid-19 being arguably the biggest fear of many Americans in 2021, we can only imagine how that has also impacted this idea of safetyism in our society today.

As pastors in 2020, "risk versus safety" was all we thought about, dreamt about, and talked about. From closing services to reopening in-person church gatherings to creating new social distancing and sanitization procedures, there seemed to be an endless debate from everyone as to what is more important: risk or safety. And furthermore, which side you were on (apparently) said everything about you. We should absolutely value the safety of those around us. It is imperative that we care for the most vulnerable in our world. Due to Covid-19, I was not able to see my ninety-nine-year-old grandmother for over seven months. It wasn't until the week before her one hundredth birthday that I was finally allowed to see her. The seven months of little to no human contact was quite detrimental to my sweet grams, but every time we would end one of our FaceTime calls she would say, "Tomorrow will be a better day." As difficult as it was during the lockdown in her senior living center, I am grateful for the safety precautions that have potentially kept my grandma from getting Covid-19.

So safety and safety precautions are important for any community. But as Christians we must also remember to live within the tension of safety and risk like the early Christians modeled.

In the first century a devastating epidemic swept through the Roman Empire that killed a quarter of the empire's population. Even the emperor Marcus Aurelius succumbed to the deadly epidemic. At its worst, some five thousand people died in a single day in Rome. Bodies were being thrown out on the Roman streets to rot. People were scared to leave their homes because the disease was thought to be so contagious.

Even if a family member was desperately in need of aid, close friends and family would not go care for their loved ones, due to the fear of getting sick. Yet the Christians were willing to risk their lives to care for the sick and dying—and many of those Christians sadly lost their own lives.

These early Christians were not extremists or adrenaline junkies. They believed it was their duty as Christians to care for the sick and dying. Why? Because Jesus had risked it all and died for them.

As Christians today, we can be quick to overvalue safety, often over our own good. With technology and modern conveniences, almost anything can be ordered straight to your front door—thank you, Amazon Prime. Because everything is basically at our fingertips, staying in places that feel safe and familiar has never been easier. Combine that with how negative the news of the outside world can seem, and it's all too easy to look for the next step that feels safest instead of looking to God. When the world looks scary and dark, we can tend to choose safety over risk. We drive home from work and immediately close our garage doors behind us and quickly run into our safe homes to stay, away from the scary world and its problems.

But the Lord has called us to a life that's way bigger than what we think is "safe." Too often, we can sit back and ignore it when we feel the Lord pulling on our hearts, asking us to trust Him. We may feel that familiar ache for a long time before we finally go into action to do what God has placed in our hearts.

Risk Versus Safety

Risk is risky! When we choose to risk, we are opening ourselves up to the possibility of loss or defeat. We could lose a job, money, relationships, reputation, or even our life when we take a risk. So, obviously, we overvalue safety. Who wants to open themselves up to such a risk? The spectrum of risk is wide and varied. You could lose a little or a lot. Some may lose friendships over political views; others may lose their life for preaching the gospel on the mission field.

I believe God built us for risk. He didn't make us in his image to hide away in our safety shelters. He created us to take a risk and show the world how good and powerful our God is. Of course, this should go without saying, but here it goes anyway: That doesn't mean all risk is of God. If you think you need to take the risk and have an affair, you're wrong. God doesn't speak outside his character. He would never tell you to do something contrary to his character, values, or commands. What God will call us to risk is our comforts and overvalued schemas. All throughout the Bible, people were presented with risk in order to follow Jesus.

Jesus told the crowds, "If anyone would come after me, let him deny himself and take up his cross and follow me. For whoever would save his life will lose it, but whoever loses his life for my sake and the gospel's will save it" (Mark 8:34–35).[3] That's a huge risk! Lose your life in order to save it. Not sure that kind of risk would make it on Wall Street, but that was the type of risk taker that Jesus was looking for.

Paul the Risk Taker

Apostle Paul is probably the most famous risk taker in the Bible. Some could argue his entire life was marked by risk. Remember in the last chapter when we discussed how Paul would "boast" of his weaknesses? He listed his résumé of weakness in 2 Corinthians:

> Five times I received at the hands of the Jews the forty lashes less one. Three times I was beaten with rods. Once I was stoned. Three times I was shipwrecked; a night and a day I was adrift at sea; on frequent journeys, in danger from rivers, danger from robbers,

danger from my own people, danger from Gentiles, danger in the city, danger in the wilderness, danger at sea, danger from false brothers; in toil and hardship, through many a sleepless night, in hunger and thirst, often without food, in cold and exposure. And, apart from other things, there is the daily pressure on me of my anxiety for all the churches. Who is weak, and I am not weak? Who is made to fall, and I am not indignant? If I must boast, I will boast of the things that show my weakness. (2 Corinthians 11:24–30)[4]

When Paul gives us a list of his "weaknesses," what he's really showing us is his willingness to risk. Paul traveled over ten thousand miles during his three missionary journeys to spread the good news. Paul knew that with each mile he was putting his life at risk for the gospel. He went into hostile environments knowing he could be beaten or arrested (multiple times), both of which he experienced. People warned Paul. Pleaded with him. Begged him not to take the risk. Paul's savage response to those who pleaded with him not to go to Jerusalem, where they knew he would be arrested: "What are you doing, weeping and breaking my heart? For I am ready not only to be imprisoned but even to die in Jerusalem for the name of the Lord Jesus" (Acts 21:13).[5]

Paul knew that his risk could cost him his life, but he went anyway. Who else is feeling like a bad Christian right now? I struggle to risk my reputation and say things as a preacher that I know people won't want to hear.

Paul isn't the only great risk taker of the Bible. In fact, the Bible is packed with courageous men and women. Another amazing risk taker of the Bible is Esther. When Queen Esther learns the evil plot of Haman to alienate all her people, the Jews, she risks her life to go and speak to the king, King Xerxes, unannounced. Not even the king's wife was allowed to interrupt the king. Such an offense was cause for death. Knowing the risk, Esther boldly proclaims, "If I perish, I perish" (Esther 4:16).[6] Can you even imagine being ready to risk your life like that?

One of my favorite risk takers in the Bible is Rahab from the book of Joshua. Rahab was a prostitute who became a biblical heroine. Yep, prostitute turned Bible superstar. In Joshua 2, Joshua sends two spies into the land of Jericho before they conquer the land. They find their way into the house of Rahab. When the king of Jericho hears she has two spies in her house, he demands that she offer them to him. She says they are not there and she does not know where they went. So the king's men go chasing out of the city walls to find the two spies, whom Rahab has hidden on her roof. After saving their lives Rahab petitions them:

> "Now then, please swear to me by the Lord that, as I have dealt kindly with you, you also will deal kindly with my father's house, and give me a sure sign that you will save alive my father and mother, my brothers

and sisters, and all who belong to them, and deliver
our lives from death." (Joshua 2:12–13)[7]

When the walls of Jericho fell, guess who was the only
remaining family? Rahab's.

"And the city and all that is within it shall be devoted to
the Lord for destruction. Only Rahab the prostitute and all
who are with her in her house shall live, because she hid the
messengers whom we sent" (Joshua 6:17).[8]

That's not even the best part of the story yet. Remember
Ruth? She was suddenly a widow alongside her mother-in-
law and sister-in-law and decided to follow her mother-in-law,
Naomi, to Moab. Another incredible risk taker who leaves her
country and people to go to an unknown land with unknown
people. Then we get the great romance story in the Bible in the
book of Ruth. Boaz and Ruth! I just swoon every time I read it.
And every girl dreams and prays for her Boaz to ride in on a white
horse and rescue her. Okay, okay, back to the point. Guess who
the mother of Boaz is? Drumroll . . . Rahab. The prostitute in
Joshua who believed in the people of Israel's God and changed
the trajectory of her entire family line. All because she took a risk.

And sorry to nerd out on you, but you have to see this!
Rahab's legacy continues. Check out the genealogy of Jesus
listed in the book of Matthew:

The book of the genealogy of Jesus Christ, the son of
David, the son of Abraham. Abraham was the father of

Isaac, and Isaac the father of Jacob, and Jacob the father of Judah and his brothers, and Judah the father of Perez and Zerah by Tamar, and Perez the father of Hezron, and Hezron the father of Ram, and Ram the father of Amminadab, and Amminadab the father of Nahshon, and Nahshon the father of Salmon, and Salmon the father of *Boaz by Rahab*, and Boaz the father of Obed by Ruth, and Obed the father of Jesse, and Jesse the father of David the king. And David was the father of Solomon by the wife of Uriah. (Matthew 1:1–6)[9]

Rahab is in the line of Jesus! Imagine how that one decision she made was worth the risk!

Risky Waters

There's a pretty epic story in the Bible where Peter walked on water with Jesus. Undoubtedly Paul heard the story, probably straight from the mouth of Peter.

It's one of those Bible stories that most people have heard of, even people who didn't grow up going to Sunday school.

The disciples were on a boat, tormented by the waves of an epic storm:

And in the fourth watch of the night he came to them, walking on the sea. But when the disciples saw him walking on the sea, they were terrified, and said, "It is a ghost!" and they cried out in fear. But immediately Jesus spoke to them, saying, "Take heart; it is I. Do not be afraid." And Peter answered him, "Lord, if it is you, command me to come to you on the water." He said, "Come." So Peter got out of the boat and walked on the water and came to Jesus. But when he saw the wind, he was afraid, and beginning to sink he cried out, "Lord, save me." Jesus immediately reached out his hand and took hold of him, saying to him, "O you of little faith, why did you doubt?" And when they got into the boat, the wind ceased. And those in the boat worshiped him, saying, "Truly you are the Son of God." (Matthew 14:22–33)[10]

Peter reminds me of myself throughout the Gospels: impulsive, tends to overreact, and occasionally puts his foot in his mouth. I can relate! He shoots off his mouth when maybe the better choice would have been to stay silent. But sometimes it's easier to ask for forgiveness than permission—a characteristic Peter and I seem to share. But what I love most about Peter is his ability to take a risk.

Peter's eyes were set on Jesus, and his heart told him to follow him into the chaos. But everything changed when Peter took his eyes off Jesus and focused on the storm, which scared him and caused him to sink. We, too, will sink when we get distracted from Jesus, our source of power. Jesus's power is stronger than our troubles! The problem for most of us is not that we don't want to give our all to Jesus. The problem is that we value safety more.

And still, even if we do take the first step like Peter, to follow God's calling, it can be all too easy to second-guess ourselves when we get out into the choppy waters of risk, too far from what we're used to. Like Peter, we may take a look around, our trust in God falling away, and start to sink.

As Peter began to panic, Jesus's words to him were a beautiful combination of rebuke and encouragement: "O you of little faith, why did you doubt?" Jesus met Peter right where he was, but He never intended to leave him there. Jesus wanted Peter to keep his eyes focused on Him, not on the problem or the what-ifs or the chaos that was screaming in his face. All Peter needed to do was to keep his eyes set on Jesus.

I love that scripture in Isaiah that says, "You keep him in perfect peace whose mind is stayed on you, because he trusts in you" (Isaiah 26:3).[11] It seems that was the Scripture Jesus was teaching as he approached Peter.

According to a piece in *Time* magazine, the average attention span has dropped from twelve seconds in the year 2000 to eight seconds today. That is less than the nine-second attention span of your average goldfish. People now generally lose concentration after eight seconds. Are you still reading? Or have I lost you every eight seconds?

No wonder we can't set our minds on Jesus.

We can't keep our eyes fixed on Him because we constantly let our attention wander. We assume that if we're doing God's will and following Jesus, it will be smooth sailing, but Jesus never promises that. What Jesus does promise you is that He'll be with you and that you can take that to heart, to not fear, to not worry, to not be anxious, to trust, to believe, to not doubt. But He never promises smooth waters.

The story of Peter walking on water in Matthew's Gospel is meant to reveal who Jesus is. But that revelation is only possible in the midst of the chaos. It takes so much more trust to follow Jesus in the middle of a storm than it does on a calm, sunny day. If Jesus had not forced the disciples to embark on this uncertain journey, they would have missed the opportunity to see God revealed in their midst.

Something about the whole experience opened their eyes to the power and ability of Jesus. Before this encounter, Jesus was just an amazing man, but now the disciples saw Him as the Messiah and worshiped him as truly the Son of God.

It's worth the risk!

The dramatic conclusion of the text is that through Peter's risk of faith (hey, even though he half failed, at least he tried!) the others saw Jesus for who He really is and worshiped Him for who He is—the One with all the power and authority.

Peter wasn't the only guy in Jesus's first-century posse to experience a storm in the middle of his faith journey. Our guy Paul also had an encounter with chaos that could have sent his contentment spiraling. Luke tells us in Acts 27 that he and Paul were undergoing a voyage to Rome, where Paul was going to have to answer further questions in court, having already been incarcerated in Caesarea for two years. The winds were not in favor of the ship, and after being tossed up and down the coast, the captain tried to avoid being dashed on the rocks and ran aground in rough surf. Paul and his fellow sailing companions ended up shipwrecked on the island of Malta. Once on the island, Paul suffered a poisonous snakebite. Look, I don't know about you, but the combo of imprisonment, harsh winds, shipwreck, and snakebite do not sound like the ingredients of contentment and trust to me. But Paul seemed unperturbed by all of this and continued to heal the sick and preach Jesus to the inhabitants of the island.

Most of the time your failures, storms, and hardships preach the gospel to the broken world around you more than your triumphs. It's incredible that even when we mess up, God can still use our mistakes and storms to reach others and shine His light through us.

There will be times when Jesus may ask us to do something risky. We may wonder how we could ever accomplish such an impossible task. We may question our ability and focus on our deficiencies. God might ask us to talk to a stranger about His saving love for them. How can we tell that person about Jesus? What if they make fun of us? What if I invite that person to church and they say no? Or what if I pray for someone to get healed, and they don't get better?

Yeah, maybe . . . or what if you risk it all and you get to walk on water with Jesus?

Risk Takers Are History Makers

Risk takers are history makers. One such great history maker was Rosa Parks, who took a risk when she refused to give up her seat on a bus in Montgomery, Alabama, in 1955, to fight racial injustice. Orville and Wilbur Wright, more famously known as "the Wright Brothers," are the inventors and pioneers of aviation who were the first to fly an airplane. Amelia Earhart was the first female to fly solo across the Atlantic Ocean. Edwin "Buzz" Aldrin and Neil Armstrong were the first astronauts to land on the moon, during their Apollo 11 NASA mission in 1969. Not to mention the risks in the automotive world by Henry Ford, and the courageous risks to protect and hide slaves like Harriet Tubman took. History is full of risk takers like these and others. And in this case, I believe history means to repeat itself.

Imagine how different our world would be today if these men and women had valued safety over risk? We were built for risk, not safety. We will be content to risk when God calls us to.

When they get to the end of their life, what kind of regrets do people hold?

I wish I would have spent more time with my family.

I wish I would have forgiven more.

I wish I would have worried less.

I wish I would have been more honest.

What do we regret? Not taking the needed risks to say no to our boss so we could have had more family dinners. We regret not taking the risk and giving up our pride to forgive the person who betrayed us. We regret not living with more faith so we could have spent less of our life sacrificing our health due to worry. We regret not telling the truth, even if it hurt a friendship.

> We only regret the things we didn't do. We regret not taking risks.
> We never regret taking a risk to love, no matter the pain. We never regret taking a risk on people, because Jesus took a risk on us when he willingly went to the cross. Risk takers are Jesus people. People who risk live content. Content people don't live with regrets; they live grateful.

Think About

- What safety in your life would you be scared to give up in order to risk for God?
- What in your life could you say would be worth the risk if God asked it of you?
- What "weaknesses," as Paul would say, in your life have actually been your willingness to risk for God?

Chapter 7

Content to Wait

f I could be a professional anything, one could argue, I would be a professional bridesmaid. I have had the distinct honor of standing with my friends as a bridesmaid fourteen times. Yes, fourteen. I could run those wedding rehearsals in my sleep. I've walked down those aisles fourteen times and have yet to trip or unsuccessfully stand in my designated spot. Unfortunately, none of these weddings took place in Costa Rica or Hawaii. At least I could have gotten a mini-vacation out of it.

Also, no, not one of those bridesmaid dresses could or would ever be worn again. It's a lie brides believe and will tell you, that the dresses selected for their bridesmaids will *certainly* be able to be used again at swanky corporate events. Yeah, no. Nope. Especially the seafoam-green tulle dress I was forced to wear by a certain bride who will remain nameless (KIRSTEN!).

I've thrown dozens of bridal showers and bachelorette parties and spent thousands of dollars on weddings, and I've loved every minute of celebrating the big moments with my dear friends. But through all these times, supporting and participating in those special occasions, I was still waiting for *my* turn.

The phrase "always a bridesmaid, never a bride" was hauntingly too close to home. I understood what it felt like to wait your whole life to meet someone to share your life with, to build a home with, and to raise a family with. I knew the harsh reality of meeting some nice guy at church, thinking he might really be "the one," only to discover he'd made a lot of girls think he was "the one" for them. I knew what it was like to wait in your twenties when the pool is supposedly swimming with potential, and each date has a spark of nervous excitement. I knew what the wait was like in your thirties when it feels like the pool has limited possibilities and you fear you will have to settle for that guy who is convinced you are the one but you are certain he is not.

I knew what it felt like to wait and wait and wait. And the longer the wait, the fewer options you had.

I wouldn't describe myself as a particularly patient person. I mean, I don't want to describe myself as impatient. But that description isn't wrong, if I'm being honest. I'm a go-getter. If I see something I want (particularly clothes), I buy it whether it's on sale or not, because I can't wait for the sale (and only sometimes have buyer's remorse). I set a goal, and I accomplish it. I believe in taking action, in forging a trail, in tackling a challenge. I love the momentum of moving forward to the next task.

For example, I don't wait until after Halloween or Thanksgiving to start listening to Christmas music or watching my favorite Christmas movies, much to the dismay of some of my friends and family members. I can't be stopped! You can't summer Christmas shame me—no way! I watch Christmas movies in July when I feel like it. And as soon as it feels "coolish" outside, I fill my car with Christmas songs. Why? Because I don't want to wait until December to feel those warm, cozy, therapeutic Christmas feelings that I love so much; I want to feel them now!

I know I'm not the only one who doesn't like to wait. Our culture is a culture of now. Sometimes it feels like everything we do is to make things quicker and more immediate. We can download an app, have something delivered to our door (I love you with all my heart, Amazon Prime, and your free two-day shipping); we can call, get a text, or reach out on social media right away. This now culture can reach every part of our lives, even the quest for love! Nothing against online dating—a lot of wonderful people have met that way—but online dating is an excellent example of how our "now culture" has tried to find new ways to speed things up, in its case the process of finding your soul mate. Having trouble meeting that special someone in your day-to-day life? Here's a list of hundreds of profiles right at your fingertips. We make snap decisions and swipe right or swipe left without any real information about someone, other than their (possibly fake) profile pic and their oh-so-impressive (and again, possibly fake) bio.

Waiting is rarely comfortable or what we want. But in spite of all the apps and deliveries that we set up to keep from waiting, it's often one of the inescapable realities of our lives. Our days are consumed by waiting. You can wake up every morning and bank on one simple truth: Today, you will have to wait for something or someone. We wait to get our morning coffee, for someone to be ready to leave the house, for the WiFi in our office to reset, for a cable repairman to arrive sometime within a six-hour window (Where are my people who've been cable-repair-guy marooned for the better part of a day?).

Days turn into months and months turn into years, and some of us feel like we have been waiting on a promise, a dream, a hope for years (maybe even our whole lives). And no one likes waiting that long.

Sometimes waiting on God's timing can almost feel like a failure. In a culture where anything seems possible if you work hard enough, a lot of what our society tells us is that if you want something and you put everything you have toward that goal, you will succeed. Our culture has an obsession with hard work and believes that you make your own destiny. And while that's an empowering message, where is the room in there for God's timing? Where is the value in honoring God when He asks you to wait on a dream you have in your heart? The stories that we tell about successful or notable people celebrate them achieving a big goal. We love the idea of the American Dream, but the waiting period of the American Dream is only talked about once the dream has come true. We like to hear about someone's struggle to make their dream a reality, but only when the story can be wrapped up in a tight little bow. Yeah, I want to hear your fantastic success story, but I want it packaged up in a thirty-minute episode with great before-and-after pictures.

Why don't we talk a lot about seasons of waiting? It's because the story feels unfinished. The stories we choose to value or focus on can make it tough when God has called us to a season of waiting. If our culture has an obsession with hard work and pursuing a goal, imagine what it feels like when God asks you to wait. It almost feels wrong when your dream seems so far away. If you're not careful, waiting can leave you feeling drained and like you failed, feeling like if you had only pushed forward a little more, maybe you would have reached your dream instead of trusting in and relying on God's perfect timing.

The Silent Years

Waiting has been one of the most significant aspects of my story, and the life and words of Apostle Paul have often helped me as I navigate through the journey and need some encouragement.

We often forget that Paul waited a lot, too. In fact, from the time Paul had his dramatic and life-altering encounter with Jesus on the road to Damascus, it would be many years before he was recognized and accepted by the apostles, those who had been with Jesus during His earthly ministry. Instead, biblical scholars call some of those years his "silent years." Paul writes that those at the center of this new Christianity didn't even know who he was. And for those who did, I think he was having to spend a lot of that time proving himself trustworthy.

I mean, let's face it: The best way to be able to walk fully into ministry is generally not to be known as the guy who stood by, watched, and approved of the executions of the very Christians he now wants to serve. That's some bad optics, to borrow a phrase from public relations and politics. In those long years, I wonder if Paul got tired in the waiting—waiting to be taken seriously, waiting to go to Jerusalem, waiting to go to all the places he longed to go. I'm sure he had a passion in his heart to talk about what Jesus had done for him, and he did—but he was in the middle of the waiting. I've asked myself, What motivated Paul to wait that long? What made him content in waiting?

I've struggled to trust what God is doing in my waiting seasons—I'm not going to lie. I've had pity parties for myself. There have been some nights when I've cried myself to sleep. I've eaten ice cream until I was sick and binge-watched TV to numb the pain. I've questioned God's goodness to me, while I watched everyone else's life progress, with mine feeling like it had been in a holding pattern for years. But after the tears dried up and the ice cream was all gone, I somehow always found my way back to trust.

And I now know why.

Because at the end of the day, I always kept a deep and strong sense of purpose. Not the kind of purpose that is all about me. But the kind that is wrapped up in and utterly consumed by what God is doing. My identity is not in situations, or people, or titles, or roles, or jobs; it finds its home in Jesus. That's my purpose. My purpose is to follow Jesus, look like Jesus, act like Jesus, and participate in Jesus's mission on earth. That means that my world can't fall apart if I lose my job, or a relationship comes to an end, or some other situation goes awry. That means that when that relationship doesn't work out (even when I'd convinced myself that God orchestrated it), I'm not devastated. My identity will never be in another person. It can only be in Jesus.

Jesus builds me stronger than I can build myself, so that when an obstacle is in my path, it's not going to break me. And that's the beauty of trusting in God's perfect timing. God never intended for you to have to carry all the weight and responsibility of your dreams and aspirations; God is right there with you guiding you to His purpose for you.

To guide our purpose there are so many things God has put in place that we can't see, so many intricate pieces that our minds can't possibly understand. God is there to make your burden light, and He wants you to put your trust in Him. It's so beautiful that God has made us part of His plan, and having a strong sense of purpose will make the waiting feel like running into your destiny! Purpose keeps you moving! It drives us! Apostle Paul waited a long time to be accepted as a leader in the church—but he didn't do it by sitting around and watching. He did it by running toward the purpose God had for his life.

But here's the secret side sauce that has to go with purpose. Any great main dish needs its super sidekick, and purpose is no exception. Chick-fil-A nuggets are awesome, but it's the Chick-fil-A sauce that makes it, right? So often we think if we can just figure out the main dish of our life, our purpose, then we'll be good to go. And it is critical to discover your purpose, particularly if you are going to live in contentment. But here it is, the complement to the savor of purpose: perseverance.

I used to do a lot of running. And, funny as it seems, there is something in running that sort of is a waiting. You're working hard, but the miles can seem to pass so slowly. You're giving it your all, but you can't make miles shorter than they are. There's just the pressing on, the willingness to wait out those miles, with the hope that you'll reach a finish line, you'll complete that circle on your Apple watch, your running app will chime to let you know you've hit your mileage.

Paul uses so many long-distance athlete kinds of references in his writing, it sometimes makes me wonder how he got his sweat on. He knows an awful lot about the mind of a runner, a boxer, a wrestler. And when he talks about waiting and that which is not yet, well, it makes for some of my favorite passages in Scripture:

Not that I have already obtained this or am already perfect, but I press on to make it my own, because

Christ Jesus has made me his own. Brothers, I do not consider that I have made it my own. But one thing I do: forgetting what lies behind and straining forward to what lies ahead, I press on toward the goal for the prize of the upward call of God in Christ Jesus. Let those of us who are mature think this way, and if in anything you think otherwise, God will reveal that also to you. Only let us hold true to what we have attained. (Philippians 3:12–16)[1]

I press on! Paul says this phrase twice in three verses. I think he wants the reader to pay attention. He knows a thing or two about pressing on in the waiting, when things are not always going the way you anticipate or hope for or dream of. I like this phrase from Paul because it makes me realize that waiting doesn't mean there won't be movement; it means that you're pushing against something and even if your progress is slow, you're moving forward. Our culture has conditioned us to believe waiting is bad, and urgency is good. Or another way to think of it is, waiting is idle, and urgency is motion. But there's always movement in the waiting. Waiting is movement. Waiting is training. Waiting is healthy. Waiting does not equal listless watching. Waiting is active trust in God.

Let's hit that again: *There's always movement in the waiting.*

Don't fall into the trap of believing there is nothing you can do when what you're longing for isn't your now. Acknowledge that you're in a waiting season in your life, but then keep on. Keep on in joy. Keep on in laughter. Keep on in doing good work, right where you are. Keep on investing in the relationships around you. Keep showing up; keep becoming your best version of yourself. Make that waiting room in your life your workout room as well, growing ever stronger and honed.

Let's think back again on Paul's waiting years, when he was launching fully into his missionary and writing period. The first thing that I notice about those years is that they took Paul completely off-course from where his education and training had been leading him. Paul tells us in Acts 22 of his pedigree. We looked at this verse in a previous chapter, but let's look closer.

He writes, "I am a Jew, born in Tarsus of Cilicia, but brought up in this city. I studied under Gamaliel and was thoroughly trained in the law of our ancestors. I was just as zealous for God as any of you are today" (Acts 22:3).[2] Did you catch that? Paul had done all the things he was supposed to do to have a great career path in Jewish circles. Gamaliel was considered the great law teacher of his day, and was a leader in the Sanhedrin, the Jewish council that oversaw all aspects of Jewish life. To have studied with Gamaliel, as Paul did, was pretty much like going to our Ivy League schools of today, as Paul would have received a top-notch education and would have been networking like a pro.

Paul must have been going up the ranks pretty fast, because by the time we read about him at the stoning of Stephen, who was a young deacon put to death for his belief in Jesus, it is

Paul who is carrying the official documentation back and forth to validate these public acts of persecution. He was trusted by people in power, he had the pedigree, he was on the fast train to success within his world.

But when Jesus interrupted his life, that all changed.

Now, I have to say, if I'd had that kind of experience, and I'd given up all the "treasures" I'd built in educational training and professional associates, I'd be expecting significant returns . . . and *fast* ones. I wouldn't want to be in any kind of state of waiting, and frankly, I think I'd feel pretty entitled to see some fast forward motion. I'd want it to be a lateral move. If I were already a "somebody" with the prominent Jewish leaders, then I'd want to be a "somebody" with the leaders of the church, the apostles. I would want to be influential and sought out and promoted quickly. Like how being a bridesmaid at all those weddings made me a wedding expert.

But that's not how it went for Paul. And there is a brilliance in it.

As it turns out, even when the apostles of the early church began to include Paul in some of the most critical issues and debates they were facing, he wasn't given some corner office and full benefits. Not that the apostles had any of that anyway. But because Paul had been walking out his faith in Jesus, not worrying about the opinion of others in the church, it made him bold when he did have time with the early leaders. He didn't hesitate to speak up on issues that were facing them. He writes about calling Peter out on a couple of things—Peter!

Peter, who walked on water (just a couple of steps, before fear had him sinking, but still!). Peter, whose confession that Jesus is the Son of God, earned him the nickname "The Rock." I think most of us would have been kissing up to Peter big-time if we'd been waiting for a position in the early church.

But not Paul. Those years of waiting had allowed him to practice living in a contentment that was focused on simply doing the next thing Jesus led him to do. No scrambling. No strategizing. No manipulating. Small, but impactful forward movements.

That contented waiting period shaped him into a power-house for preaching the gospel. Paul was so clear about his purpose. And he became known for not holding back when he was protecting the purity in the message of Jesus. Paul was ultimately entrusted by the apostles to help carry messages to sprouting churches across the region. Even though we don't know a lot about what Paul was up to, in those years between his conversion and finally being vetted by the apostles, we do know he was sharing his testimony and was actively engaging others in conversations of faith. He tells us, "I was personally unknown to the churches of Judea that are in Christ. They only heard the report: 'The man who formerly persecuted us is now preaching the faith he once tried to destroy.' And they praised God because of me" (Galatians 1:22–24).[3] *Because of him.* He saw through his mission.

When you find yourself in a place where you feel pretty sure of your purpose, but you're still wrestling discontent, it's time to watch what you're dipping that purpose in. Are you swirling it in a dish of pity, or are you enhancing your purpose with perseverance? Perseverance is waiting, yes, just like we've been talking about in this chapter, but it's the kind of waiting that I mean when we talk about being content in waiting. Perseverance is *active* waiting.

We don't like to talk about perseverance. When I hear the term, I can always feel that little whiff of hesitation hit my soul, because I think, Oh, here it comes. Instead of feeling like I'm getting closer to my breakthrough, I'm going to have to hunker down, buckle up, and wait some more. But purpose blended with perseverance equals patience. That's how I can stay in a place of contentment while I wait.

Paul's not the only person in Scripture who practically had a Ph.D. in waiting. Joseph in the Old Testament had big dreams as a kid (as in the prophecy kind of dream, dreams in which he was a leader), but it was years and years before any of that came to pass, with a lot of challenges along the way. Joseph grabbed hold of his purpose and never let go, even when his circumstances (like being betrayed by his brothers, falsely accused of rape and then imprisoned) were essential factors in the waiting. He held on to that purpose and kept it dipped in perseverance. And when the door opened for Joseph to walk into the fullness of his dream, he was ready.

Elizabeth, in the New Testament, waited and waited for a baby. And waited some more. And frankly, it all looked pretty bleak. Her husband was up there in age, and she'd probably attended way more baby showers for everyone else than seemed fair. But one day, her husband Zechariah was serving in the temple, and he learned from an angel that Elizabeth was going to have a baby. All the waiting was finally over!

Or . . . was it?

Actually, she had nine more months of waiting in front of her. And then check this out. There's this obscure little verse in the book of Luke, tucked away in the middle of all this excitement that Elizabeth was pregnant. It says, "When his [Zechariah's] time of service [in the temple] was completed, he returned home. After this his wife Elizabeth became pregnant and *for five months remained in seclusion*" (Luke 1:23–24, clarification mine, emphasis added).[4] Did you catch it? This is a woman who has waited all her adult life to get pregnant. And once she does, she's not out at the grocery store telling everyone. She wasn't going to the temple each week, showing off her expanding waistline. It sounds to me like she and Zechariah kept things on the down-low for five long months after their child, John, was conceived.

Why?

Why would God have her wait any longer?

Here's my opinion, based on some scripture just a little further down in the chapter. After Zechariah's encounter with the angel, after Elizabeth gets pregnant, after she goes into more waiting by being in seclusion, an angel visits Elizabeth's cousin Mary. The angel lets Mary know that she is going to have a child, the son of God. Mary is understandably confused by this. " 'How will this be,' Mary asked the angel, 'since I am a virgin?' " (Luke 1:34).[5]

Seems like a fair question to me. . . .

"The angel answered, 'The Holy Spirit will come on you, and the power of the Most High will overshadow you. So the holy one to be born will be called the Son of God. Even Elizabeth your relative is going to have a child in her old age, and she who was said to be unable to conceive is in her sixth month. For no word from God will ever fail" (Luke 1:35–37).[6]

There it is, a little nod toward all that waiting Elizabeth has been doing. Mary must not have known about Elizabeth's pregnancy at this point, Elizabeth being all tucked up at the house and all. So the wait behind the reveal of Elizabeth's condition had a purpose. It served as a sign to Mary, who knew of her cousin's longing for a child, who knew that the years had passed without any indication of hope. For Mary to find out in this moment confirmed all the angel had been telling her.

How cool is that?

All that waiting, even the waiting of those months to announce that the pregnancy test had turned positive for Elizabeth and Zechariah, it wasn't random. It wasn't without meaning. It meant even more, and it's no wonder then that Mary quickly makes her way to Elizabeth's town and house. She busts in the door, that door that has been keeping Elizabeth from the public eye. And when Elizabeth hears Mary's voice calling for her, the baby Elizabeth is carrying gives a jump for joy. In that moment, all the years of waiting, all the wondering why and when, come together in a symphony of confirmation and celebration.

There is power in the wait. There is purpose in the wait. There is reward in the persevering.

I might have fourteen hideous bridesmaid dresses in my closet, but they are not signs of what I don't have. They're reminders that I'm living on purpose, and my life is shaping up just fine. When I see those bridesmaid dresses, they remind me of the friendships I've invested in that God has placed on my life. It's an honor that fourteen wonderful people found so much value in our relationship that they wanted me to stand beside them on one of the most important days of their lives. And at just the right time, my friends will get their deserved payback, and I'll pick out a bridesmaid dress for them that I'll tell them they can totally wear again.

Surprise, the wait is over! My bridesmaids got what was coming for them. Kidding! Actually they looked gorgeous in their cute black dresses (not seafoam green). You see, during the writing of this book the unexpected happened for me: I met my now husband. What started as a happy birthday message he sent to me on Instagram slowly evolved into a beautiful, redemptive love story. Yep, he slid into my DMs, and I fell for it hook, line, and sinker. Garrison and I met through our church, and a year and some change later we were married on New Year's Eve.

I love my story of waiting. I was thirty-nine years old on our wedding day. Basically a death sentence for most gals, but for me it was the beautiful reminder that God writes the best stories. I love the journey of waiting I walked through to get to marriage. You never appreciate the value of something as much as when you have to wait for it.

Think About

- What have you been waiting for? How long has it been?
- Do you think of yourself as a patient person? Or, like me, do you find waiting to be super-hard?
- Do you think contentment and waiting can coexist?

Chapter 8

Content in Where I Am

t is so easy in our culture today to be dissatisfied. We want what other people have. We're always longing for the next best (and new) thing. We're convinced that everyone else's life is better than ours. That proverbial other man's grass is always greener. This cultural discontent has become the narrative of our lives.

Much of our cultural dissatisfaction is due to our consumer mentality. We are a consumer culture! We all probably have more of a consumer mind than we do a biblical mind, and we don't even realize it.

I spend more time searching for a show on Netflix than actually watching anything. It blows my mind that I can have all these streaming services—Netflix, Hulu, Amazon Prime—and still not be able to find anything to watch. Is that because there are no shows to watch? No! It's because I have developed, and become conditioned to having, a consumer mind. I want to watch something that meets all my expectations. Not that movie—I'm not crazy about that lead actor. Not that one—it's not funny enough. Not that one—I don't like the soundtrack.

Not that one—I'm not in the mood for sci-fi. I have conditioned my mind to think that everything is here to entertain me.

We ditch relationships the moment they stop feeding our
perceived needs. Why? Because we go into relationships with
a consumer mindset. What can this person do for me? How
can they improve my life, my personality, my dreams? Whoa
whoa whoa! You're not dating Jesus. No person has the power
to do what Jesus does.

And let's face it: We're also in an era of church-shopping
with a consumer mindset as well. It's argued that 96 percent
of church growth today is transfer growth. Meaning: People
are leaving their churches to arrive at a new one. This makes
me sad for two reasons: Christians are church hopping more
than I realized, and the church is not reaching the lost like we
should. We have made church more about us and less about
the mission of Jesus, which is to go out and share the good
news. Churches should never be on the decline; if we're called
to be missional, they should be ever increasing because new
believers are coming all the time.

Why so much church-transfer growth, then? We're wired
to want the next best thing. When shopping for a new car, we
want all the new bells and whistles and exciting features (half
of which we never learn to use or forget to use). We want the
new fashion trends and stick our nose up at last year's fashion
craze. When we get bored with our once favorite restaurant,
coffee shop, relationship, or church when it no longer feeds our
need for new and exciting . . . then we go on the hunt for our

new favorite spot. This is the embedded fabric of the American way. We choose churches based on our desires and preferences. Is the worship contemporary, yet traditional? Is the preacher deep, yet relatable? Is the children's ministry like Disneyland with a fairy dust of Jesus? Is parking easy? Is the service timely, yet not overly structured or liturgical?

Now, don't get me wrong. I love being part of a church that has music I love and people I resonate with and teaching that challenges me. But what if I lived in a community that only had a couple of churches and neither of them met my "expectations"? Would I still go? Would I still obey God's word to seek out a community of faith and be in the "habit" of meeting together? (See Hebrews 10:25 if you need some vetting on this.)

A consumer approach to our relationships, a consumer approach to our faith communities, will leave us feeling empty and unsatisfied, exposed to the enemy's attacks of purposelessness and downcast feelings.

Paul also addressed this, with the church at Ephesus. Ephesus was a community that had a form of spirituality, but it wasn't a form redeemed through Jesus Christ. It was a town that worshiped through idols and sorcery, selling false gods and promises to people. If they just bought this or that household idol, then they could make circumstances bend to their favor. Paul wanted to free them from those kinds of fleshly strongholds, and he talked to them about the importance of a new mindset: "You were taught, with regard to your former way of life, to put off your old self, which is being corrupted by its deceitful desires; to be made new in the attitude of your minds; and to put on the new self, created to be like God in true righteousness and holiness" (Ephesians 4:22–24).[1]

We don't need new churches, church communities, or pastors. We need to put on a new mind.

Self-Talk

Have you ever listened or taken inventory of the running self-talk in your head? It would probably terrify us to know what we really thought about ourselves if we took the time to catalog it. We're so used to hearing ourselves say:

"That was a really stupid thing to say."
"You'll never look as good as her."
"Why do you do that all the time?"
"You're such an idiot."

I'm a firm believer in the power of thoughts that eventually shape themselves into words. And our words sure have power over us, don't they? How do we get our minds to think right, so our thoughts and words match up with what God says about us? We must get a new mind. Well, actually a better way of saying it is, we don't need a new mind, we need a more *biblical* mind.

We have to saturate our minds with God's word. That's the only way we can put on our new self, new mind, right mind.

Sure, we can spend more time reading self-help books, and listening to podcasts about improving our lives, or talking to counselors. But as good as those things can be, if we spend more time on that than we engage in the Bible, then we will remain discontent with where we are. Always looking for the grass that appears to be greener anywhere other than where we are right now. I have never believed more in the need for reading Scripture daily! If I'm going to put on the "new self" that Jesus has offered me, then I will have to be committed to listening to God's word every single day. The old self is the one who has negative self-talk racing through her mind. The new self has God-talk coursing through her veins. We can't live this life in victory apart from God's word. The Bible teaches me to know what it means to be *content in who I am* and *content in where I am right now*.

Two of the most significant self-talk lies I have had to overcome are:

Who I am is not enough.
Where I am is not good enough.

Which lies about yourself do you need to overcome? Really. Stop just a moment here and think about the two biggest lies you hear echo around in your heart and head. Recognize that they are there. That's the first part of the battle.

As I've wrestled with those two statements that are my biggest self-talk lies, I've had to replace the language that I found there. And no, I'm not talking about telling myself more lies to cover these self-talk lies. I've experienced people who, in an effort to overcome a self-talk lie, have told themselves another lie to cover the first one. If you're wrestling with an addiction, say, to alcohol, and you've been beating yourself up about it with the lie "I'm such a failure," the replacement for that lie is not a lie that says, "I don't have an alcohol problem." The lie of telling yourself that you're a failure needs to be uncovered. And underneath that lie is the truth that you are worthy. And because you are worthy, there is a further truth that you are worth getting the help you need to get you beyond this alcohol addiction that is leaving you feeling like a failure.

Let's uncover those self-talk lies with the truth and let the truth do its work. Get with a trusted mentor, pastor, or counselor. Tell them the words that swirl through your heart and prevent contentment from residing there. And then, with prayer and guidance and wisdom, sweep out the corners of your soul, taking down those cobwebs of discouragement and isolation and falsehood.

Here's how I've been walking this out, in replacing the two biggest self-talk lies I've battled.

Replace "Who I Am Is Not Enough" with "I Am Content in Who I Am"

Isn't it funny how the very thing we pray for is often the thing we complain about or pray for God to take from us? Don't get mad at God when He answers your prayers—you prayed for what you're walking in.

People ask me a lot what it's like to be a woman in leadership and ministry. My answer is usually "It's awesome! I love it!" When they ask me about the challenges of ministry as a woman, my answer has become less and less about being accepted as a female preacher or leader—that's becoming less of an issue in our culture today. The challenge for me over the years was more about being a single woman in ministry. For some reason, I think people would prefer if a woman is going to preach, that there be a man in her life, keeping her in check. Hey, I didn't blame them. I thought that would be nice, too. But that wasn't my story for a long time, and I believe God prepared me for the long season of ministry as a single woman even as a young girl.

I grew up in church as a pastor's kid and basically started working in the church office as soon as I could walk and talk. They let me volunteer in the nursery when I was seven . . . seven?! Why would they let me take care of babies when I was still a baby myself? I was volunteering in the church office after school from kindergarten on.

People in our church noticed how invested I was in the church and probably recognized that God was developing something in me even at a young age. They would look at me and ask, "Are you going to grow up and marry a pastor one day?"

"No, I'm going to be the pastor," I would reply.

Oh man, what an obnoxious little kid I was.

I'm sure I had no clue what I was saying, but God knew what He had deposited in me and would be developing in me all my life.

As I continued to grow up in church, I developed a deep hunger for God and desired to live out the life He designed for me. So I was the idiot who at youth camps and revival services prayed:

"Use me, Lord."

"Do whatever you want with my life, it's all yours."

"I'll go anywhere you want."

"Not my will, but Yours be done in every part of my life."

If you have been on this journey any amount of time, you, too, have prayed similar prayers. I think built into every human soul is a desire and fire to be used by God in a big way. God's purposes course through our veins, and we just want to GO for God! However, we aren't always aware of what it's going to look like or mean.

The life I lived for nearly two decades was a lot of what I prayed for. I didn't want to be someone's wife who just occasionally got to do ministry. I wanted to live out what God had equipped me for since I was a little girl. But that thing I desired as a young girl at times was the most challenging part of ministry for me—to do it alone. And because I did ministry alone for so many years, it often spurred those cruel echoes in my heart that I wasn't enough.

While I had some awesome women in my life who are also in ministry, not many of them were in my situation. A lot of them were married to their ministry partner. They worked together. They ministered together. And, as it turned out, because there weren't a lot of women out there, at least in my circles, who were single and pastoring, I sometimes felt myself measuring what I did up against those who were in different ministries, with different situations, and I would find myself wondering if I was doing enough, if I measured up, if I would be more effective if I were doing life and ministry with a man in my life.

I'm just being honest here.

At times, that wave of telling myself I'm not enough, that if I was, the ministry would be this size and there would be a spouse involved and I would be getting this or that opportunity, well, sometimes I let that wave knock me down in the past. I let it sweep over me, and it took that mocking lie of "not enough" down deep into my marrow.

But God taught me how to push back. He taught me how to sing a new song over myself, the one He sings over me. Let this wash over you instead: "For the Lord your God is living among you. He is a mighty savior. He will take delight in you with gladness. With his love, he will calm all your fears. He will rejoice over you with joyful songs" (Zephaniah 3:17).[2] Even when I felt like I wasn't enough, God delighted over me. Even when I questioned how I measured up, God was rejoicing over me in song. And even when I feared that I wasn't all I should be, God calmed that.

What if? What if you would commit this scripture to heart and speak it over yourself when that self-talk lie wants to take center stage? How would things change if you simply started declaring this over yourself? You've got nothing to lose except the self-talk lie. And you've got so much to gain.

I have the great honor and privilege to pastor and lead young people. I'm the young adult pastor at my church, Capital Church. I get to preach, disciple, lead, and love people! It's the best job in the world! I consider it an honor to pastor people because I am invited into the most intimate moments of their lives. I'm called on when there is a loss or death, to help comfort, but I'm also given the joy of celebrating life's other significant moments, too: weddings, births, promotions, healings! What an incredible honor to walk with someone through every stage of life.

Now, it's not the only thing I prayed for, this thing I'm known for, being a pastor. But I'm not even close to the end of my story. So I've learned to not concern myself with what I'm not yet or what I don't have yet. I've learned to lean into every season God so graciously prepared for me, believing as He did that He had made me enough for every single season.

We never stay in the same season forever (praise break!!!!), but we do need to learn to be content in where we are right now. Realize and thank God that you are built for the season you are in. God has been developing it in you over the entire course of your life. He doesn't waste a single season of your life. He makes you enough. And you just might have prayed for the place you are in, so you better live it up! Enjoy it! Celebrate it! Because just like any season, it will change. And then He will make you enough again to tackle that new season and that new role.

Replace "Where I Am Is Not Good Enough" with "I Am Content in Where I Am Right Now"

One of the biggest lessons of my life thus far has been learning to be content right where I am and not rushing to get ahead of myself. Have you ever felt behind in life? When you do, you're tempted to jump ahead and try and make things fit and work together, only to discover that you could have just stayed right where you were and still made it to where you needed to be at just the right time. I vehemently dislike the "just the right time" expression. I know, I know; God is never late and never too early, He's always right on time. But come on, waiting on that "just the right time" is maddening, isn't it?

I don't like being late. I think I get it from my dad. He and I, we're the ones who aren't just going to show up on time, we're probably going to be a little early. But I was born into a relatively arrive-late kind of family. My brother and sister seemed to miss my dad's on-time gene. I realized very early on that the only way I was going to be on time for anything was to wake up extra early and ask my dad to take me. So that meant that instead of attending the later church service, I would have to get up at an ungodly hour of the morning to get ready and go with my dad to pre-service prayer and attend the early service with him. That was the only way I wouldn't be late to church.

Maybe it was because I spent most of my childhood waiting for my brother and sister to hurry up so we wouldn't be late—but as I grew up, I struggled with God's sense of timing. I often felt the things of my life were late, or that I was behind what should be. Sometimes it felt like God was over somewhere, distracted by getting things done in His other kids' lives, and I was marooned on the couch, just waiting to go to church.

Right after high school, I spent two years doing an internship. My first year I was interning at my local church; my second year was spent in Washington, D.C., working on Capitol Hill. By the time I had finished the two years, I was itching to get to college and *finish* it already. I felt so behind. My other friends of the same age were already halfway through college, and I hadn't even started. I felt that pressure, that urgency to somehow catch up to my age peers. I appreciated the value of the two previous years and knew they had been foundational for me, but I couldn't wait any longer. I needed to get going. My first semester of college, I jammed in as many courses and credits as my advisor would allow. I averaged 19–22 credits a semester while working at Banana Republic (and spending all of my money on clothes—do you see a theme here?) and volunteering at my church. Plus, I enrolled in summer school every summer so I could graduate with my bachelor's degree in political science in three years and one summer semester. I had to catch up!

But this nagging sense of "feeling behind" didn't end after college. It progressed to something even worse. I was wishing away my present, pushing for a fuzzy future. I didn't understand or appreciate the time I was living in right then, and I failed to see how every season was necessary for the next.

After college I immediately went to work for the governor of Idaho—and for a recent political science graduate, that was quite an awesome opportunity. It was everything I'd worked so hard for in college; all that hurrying and catching up seemed to be paying off finally. But then I became worried I was already behind in my career because my friends were applying to law schools and graduate schools and already planning their next steps, and I was working 7 a.m. to 7 p.m. and wondering what I was doing with my life.

That "you're behind" voice crept up again and again and made me lose focus on what was right in front of me. After some time in the state capitol, I took a new job in Washington, D.C., working for the National Prayer Center, a ministry of prayer to congressional leaders, their staffs, and their families. It blended my passions for government and the church quite nicely. I thought, This is it! I will finally, definitely feel like I'm right where I'm supposed to be! But, once again, that self-talk lie came creeping back in. I discovered, rather quickly, that I was worried all over again that I wasn't getting ahead like others my age. Now many of my friends were finishing graduate school and stepping into careers they had been planning for, and here I was walking around D.C. wondering if I had missed the boat.

What I didn't realize then was that God was building in me the tools and qualifications I would need for the next season He had for me. Here I was in D.C., a young, bold twenty-something girl, and I was interacting with senatorial and congressional leaders and their staffs through my work with the National Prayer Center. I would courageously ask senators if we could pray for them. They always obliged, and standing in the halls of Congress, I would lead out in prayer for our leaders, just as 1 Timothy 2:2 admonishes all Christians to do.

I was around some of the most influential people in the world and learning to lead. And much of the time, I was more focused on what I thought I was missing, how my timeline wasn't lining up with my peers'. I'd created a calendar of fictitious milestones for my life that was outpacing my contentment. What I didn't realize was that God needed to instill in me a compassion and boldness to lead influential people. I was exactly where I was supposed to be, but I let a self-talk lie make me think I was lost.

During my season in Washington, D.C., I began my graduate studies and finally received my master's of divinity in practical theology. Having recently finished seminary (and with a lot of questions to God, wondering what He was doing with my life), I was asked to help lead and pastor a thriving community in Beverly Hills, California. At first, I said absolutely not. I was far more comfortable in a room of political thinkers than I would be in a room full of "really, really ridiculously good-looking people."

But what I was starting to realize was that my years in D.C. had been crucial for my next assignment of pastoring influential people in Hollywood. I was not easily starstruck; God had instilled that in me in D.C. (Unless I ever meet Andre Agassi. . . . Then I might completely lose all social awareness.) In D.C., I spent every day around arguably the most powerful, elite, educated, and highly intelligent people from around the world. Not much fazed me after that—instead, I had built a love and compassion for them. So by the time I found myself standing in front of a room on the opposite coast of the nation, in Hollywood, leading a group of arguably the most beautiful, talented, and famous people I had ever encountered in my life—I wasn't enamored. God had been building, for years, a grace in me to help lead these people. If I had never gone to D.C., I'm not sure I would have ever been chosen to go to Beverly Hills. And the story doesn't end there! The biggest challenge for me in Beverly Hills turned out to be the thing God was building in me for my next assignment. The years I spent in California were some of the most formative yet challenging of my life.

I often felt isolated and alone, leading without a spouse. It was always my biggest prayer to God to send me help. God was always helping me, but He was doing something in me greater than my prayer for help. He was building a capacity in me in this season to be able to lead by myself.

A few years ago, I moved back to where I grew up, Boise, where I am now the pastor of our college and young adult ministry. It is a thriving community! I don't think I ever would have had the courage to say yes or the capacity to lead if it wasn't for God building that courage and capacity in me in Beverly Hills. Each season built upon the next. And each season and place was crucial for the next.

All that time I spent thinking I might be in the wrong place at the wrong time, and yet in God's plan, I was always right on time and right where He wanted me. God is never late. He's never too early. He's always right on time. But instead of focusing so much on the timing, why don't we learn to be okay with where we are right now? Don't rush to leave a season because it is uncomfortable, stretching, or scary. It might be building something in you that is crucial for the next assignment. There's a purpose for where you are. Don't rush to leave it.

The Secret to Contentment

If someone offered me a guaranteed secret for how to live content—you better believe I would take it.

Remember that *Friends* episode where Monica desperately tries to figure out how to get the secret chocolate chip cookie recipe from Phoebe's grandma? Phoebe's grandmother made her swear never to give up the secret recipe. Phoebe finally gives in to Monica's begging and says she will get the recipe, only to discover it was burned in a fire. Monica spends days and some twenty batches of cookies trying to figure out the secret to the unbelievably good cookies. She almost gives up, until she thinks to ask if any other family member might have the recipe. Phoebe remembers that her grandmother got the recipe from a French friend, "Nestlé Toulouse." Right then Monica realizes that Phoebe's grandmother never had a secret recipe but instead used the recipe from the Nestlé Toll House chocolate chip bag. I'm laughing just thinking about this hilarious episode.

The lengths we go to in order to discover the secret of things. And here we have Paul giving us the secret to contentment. Paul tells us he learned the secret to being content . . . even when his heart was wanting:

> Not that I am speaking of being in need, for I have learned in whatever situation I am to be content. I know how to be brought low, and I know how to abound. In any and every circumstance, I have learned the secret of facing plenty and hunger, abundance and need. I can do all things through him who strengthens me. (Philippians 4:11–13)[3]

My favorite part of these verses is the word *learned*. It implies that it wasn't something Paul was born with. He had to learn through experiences, both negative and positive, how to practice and walk in contentment. Learning anything new takes practice. You can't decide one day that you are going to play the piano. You have to learn to play the piano. And in order to learn, you have to practice every day. Growing up, like a lot of kids, my mom put me in piano lessons. I loved the idea of one day becoming a world-renowned pianist. Maybe I would play in the grand Carnegie Hall and be known as the next Beethoven. There was just one little problem to this far-fetched fantasy. I loathed practicing piano.

Another way we need to learn to be content in who we are and where we are is by remembering the law of opposites. We need to remind ourselves that just because something isn't good (or what we think is good) doesn't mean God's not in it or working. There is such a thing as unity of opposites. Take electricity, for example. Electricity has to have both a positive and a negative charge to work. Even atoms contain protons and electrons, which are unified but ultimately contradictory forces. For those that are married, you know opposites really do attract. One of the biggest shocks for me when my husband, Garrison, and I got married was to discover we had totally opposite love languages. Garrison's love languages are quality time and physical touch. Quality time doesn't even register on my love language test. Quality time? I was thirty-nine years old when I was married. The only thing I ever had quality time with was my dog and, sadly, he died. My love language is acts of service, and my husband has informed me I should choose another love language because it's too hard. Just because we express and receive love in different ways doesn't mean there isn't the unity of opposites operating in our marriage. God uses both of us, individually, to help each other grow. God knows we need the law of opposites.

Take it from Paul: You play contentment against discontentment. Paul often takes things that we typically think of as contradictory and uses them to show just how God uses it all. He says, "That's why, for Christ's sake, I delight in weaknesses, in insults, in hardships, in persecutions, in difficulties. For when I am weak, then I am strong" (2 Corinthians 12:10).[4] I mean, who says that? Pleasure in weakness and insults and persecutions and difficulties? And who says that weakness means you're strong?

Paul. That's who says it. Paul. And he's showing us that principle I was just talking about, the unity of opposites, the way God can take the things we see as deficits, as discontents, and make us all the stronger and more joyful for them. Paul goes even further in explaining how God takes things that seem opposite and uses them for His purposes:

> But God chose what is foolish in the world to shame the wise; God chose what is weak in the world to shame the strong; God chose what is low and despised in the world, even things that are not, to bring to nothing things that are, so that no human being might boast in the presence of God. And because of him you are in Christ Jesus, who became to us wisdom from God, righteousness and sanctification and redemption, so that, as it is written, "Let the one who boasts, boast in the Lord." (1 Corinthians 1:27–31)[5]

We must allow the word of God to replace our old self with our new self—which replaces our consumer mind with a biblical mind so that we can know the joy of being content.

Think About ───────────────────────────

- What are you most discontented with about yourself right now? Is it how you look, who your relationships are with, that secret sin that no one knows about and you know is causing you harm? Who can you be honest with about that discontent you have in yourself? Who can help you process it? I'm not talking about someone who will tell you "Oh, no, you shouldn't feel that way! You're awesome!" and then move on. I'm talking about someone who can constructively help you unpack what has you struggling with being content in yourself.

- How affected are you by the timelines our culture puts in place about what age we should have a degree by, what age we should be married by, when we should have our first child, when we should buy our first house? Do you find yourself worried and concerned and discontent because of those timelines?

- Now find something you are content about in yourself. I mean it! Don't tell me there's nothing. If you're drawing breath, then you can at least find contentment in your ability to breathe. You can at least find contentment in your epic ability to nap. Practice a dialog of gratefulness for how God created you. After all, when you diss the creation, you diss the Creator. Honor God with what you say about yourself.

- Reflect on the life you've lived to this point and draw out the timing and the circumstances that you can now see God was using. Maybe it's that move you had back in elementary school that was so tough at the time, but now you see it led you to meet the person who's been one of your best friends ever since. Now pay that observation forward, projecting that awareness of how God worked things together for you in the past with the belief that He will do it again in your future.

Chapter 9

Content with
What I Have

'm not great at losing. You could say I'm competitive. I blame my older brother, Krist, who told me repeatedly, "Wildes win."

Luckily my sister and I were both athletic like our older brother, and we loved sports! But we loved winning the most! I'll never forget my eighth-grade basketball championship game when the varsity coach of the high school I would be attending in the fall came to watch his future prospects. I saw him in the crowd and knew I needed to make a big impression, so I stole the ball and ran it down court for a winning layup (well, I'm not sure it was the winning basket, but that's the way I like to remember it). The varsity coach came up to me after the game and said, "Wilde, I'm excited to see you next year." It felt like the biggest and best moment of my life.

However, I didn't always win. Even though basketball was my primary sport, I also played volleyball and tennis, and ran track. Track was another sport my brother was annoyingly good at. I typically played the same positions in sports as my brother, and I ran the same heats as him in track and field.

So the comparison was real and rough. Krist was fast. And I wanted to be just like him.

In fourth and fifth grade, the goal was always to make the annual city track meet, which was held on the track at Boise State University. You had to win at districts to make it, but it was the big show!

It was time for my 100-yard dash sprint. I don't remember my brother at very many of my basketball games or track meets when I was growing up because he typically had his own games or practices at the same time. But this day, I will never forget. Krist was in the stands. He had won this very race, on this very track, five years earlier. I couldn't let him down. After all, "Wildes win."

There is absolutely nothing more nerve-wracking than the start of a track meet race. Getting your feet in the blocks. Checking your hands on the lines. Listening for the gun to go off. Making sure you push out of the blocks fast enough. That day felt like even more pressure as I got in the starting position.

Ready.

Set.

Start.

"False start. Come back."

The runner next to me had false-started, and my heart raced as we reset.

Take two.

Ready.

Set.

Start. Another racer false-started. I wasn't the only nervous runner that day.

Take three. I could feel my head pounding and my mind was racing.

As we loaded back into the blocks, I was terrified I would be the one to false-start this time.

Ready.

Set.

GO.

Everyone went, and it felt like I was moving through molasses as I got out of the blocks to run for that finish line. From the get-go, I was in dead last place. I had never run so fast in all my life to such minimal results. I caught up to two other girls, but there were still five more runners in front of me as we approached the finish line. The weight of this impending defeat was seemingly unbearable for me as I thought of my brother sitting in the stands watching his little sister embarrassing his legacy. So I did what any mature and young girl of good character would do: I faked pulling a hammy as I crossed the finish line in fifth place.

I grabbed my hamstring muscle and fell to the ground. I'm not even sure I knew that I was faking a hamstring injury. I had seen others fall to the ground and hold that part of their leg in pain in other races. So it made sense in the moment. The trainers came rushing to my aide, to check my leg. They gave me some ice, and to really sell it, I limped all the way up the stands to where my family was sitting. It wasn't until years later—we're talking years, not until my twenties—that I admitted to my family that I had faked the injury. Of course, we all got a good laugh out of it, but I spent a lot of years feeling like such a failure for losing that race. There is something built deep within the human soul that stubbornly refuses to accept loss or failure.

Content to Lose

Following Jesus looks and feels like an upside-down way of life. Paul demonstrates that loss in God's kingdom is considered gain. We can't even fathom this thought. Loss is greater than gain? No Way. Getting. Achieving. Accumulating. I believe it was Socrates who once said, "Contentment is natural wealth, luxury is artificial poverty." It is a never-ending cycle of more. We want more wealth, more fame, more friends . . . more, more, more. There's nothing intrinsically wrong with desiring more for your life. We should want more. But all our desiring for more should go beyond monetary items. The more we should be after is more contentment.

To Paul, and more importantly to Jesus, you didn't need more to be content.

Paul says in Philippians 3,

> But whatever gain I had, I counted as loss for the sake
> of Christ. Indeed, I count everything as loss because
> of the surpassing worth of knowing Christ Jesus my

Lord. For his sake I have suffered the loss of all things and count them as rubbish, in order that I may gain Christ and be found in him, not having a righteousness of my own that comes from the law, but that which comes through faith in Christ, the righteousness from God that depends on faith—that I may know him and the power of his resurrection, and may share his sufferings, becoming like him in his death, that by any means possible I may attain the resurrection from the dead. (Philippians 3:7–11)[1]

Paul had every reason to have confidence in what he had, what he had earned and learned, and in who he was in society. Yet he says, "But whatever gain I had, I counted as loss for the sake of Christ."

Paul was okay to lose. To him, anything and everything other than Jesus Himself was a loss. If you have Jesus, you're a winner. You have all you need. You have no lack. But if you don't find everything you need in Jesus and Jesus alone, then it's all a loss. Why loss? Why couldn't Paul just be chill and consider all his old credentials and résumé as additional gain? Seems extreme, Paul.

Let's be clear. Having a good résumé is not bad. Having an education is not bad. Being influential is not bad. Being zealous for what you do is not bad. Paul isn't saying those things are in and of themselves bad. But what he is saying is that compared to the worth of knowing Jesus, none of those things matter or could ever compare; they are rubbish. We don't necessarily think the things we desire or the résumé items we're trying to build up are insignificant; marrying the right person, having a certain number of children (via the way we desire them to come: natural birth, C-section, in-vitro, adoption, or foster care), having the perfect job, and having lots of influence (especially becoming Instagram famous) are important potential components in our lives. We have convinced ourselves that all these things are the gains we are owed as Jesus followers.

But what if following Jesus means you're going to lose all those gains? What if you take a stand for something on your social media account that you feel is Jesus-honoring . . . and people decide to unfollow you? What if you decide that you need to have a serious talk with that guy you're getting serious about, because he's not really all that committed to faith . . . and he seriously breaks up with you over it? Are you content to lose in situations like that? Are you content to lose for what is right?

I've got to be honest. It's taken a long time for me to get content with that kind of losing. It creeps up on me from time to time, the notion that since I'm in ministry and I'm trying to live my life right and I'm trying to make good choices, well then, Jesus kinda-sorta owes me.

Owes? When did Jesus start having to owe us anything?

The difficult truth to accept is that Jesus doesn't owe us anything. We live like we are owed everything, and on our timetable, and by golly, it better come in the exact way we prayed, fasted, and fantasized for it to happen. But nothing in Scripture and nothing about God makes Him our genie in a bottle who does what we want Him to do. God is so gracious and good that He has welcomed us to be participants in His rescue operation plan for His good, good earth, but we're not owed anything. We've been given Jesus when we don't deserve it. And instead of giving our entire lives to love and serve Jesus, we live like Jesus owes it to us to show us how much He loves and wants to serve our needs and greatest desires.

Any notion I might have that I can exchange my "good" behavior for an IOU from Jesus gets all turned sideways when I peer again into the words of Paul. Here's part of my (appropriate) girl pastor crush on Paul: He is a straight shooter. He doesn't hold back. He doesn't try to pretty things up to make me *feel* better. He says it bluntly, to make *me* better.

Paul slaps us in the face (and boy oh boy do we need it) with Philippians 3:8: "Indeed, I count everything as loss because of the surpassing worth of knowing Christ Jesus my Lord. For his sake I have suffered the loss of all things and count them as rubbish, in order that I may gain Christ."

I Can Do All Things Doesn't Mean Everything

It is one of those misused and misquoted verses of the Bible. "I can do all things through him who strengthens me" (Philippians 4:13).[2] When we take this verse out of context, we tend to believe the "all things" part means whatever we need or want to accomplish. Thus we interpret that scripture to mean that we will have success in whatever we choose to do. Whether I want to run a marathon, run for president, or run away from my family . . . I can do all things through Jesus, who has strengthened me.

In order to get a fuller understanding of the context behind Paul's words, we need to remind ourselves of the few verses before Paul says "I can do all things through him":

"Not that I am speaking of being in need, for I have learned in whatever situation I am to be content. I know how to be brought low, and I know how to abound. In any and every circumstance, I have learned the secret of facing plenty and hunger, abundance and need" (Philippians 4:11–12).[3]

Paul knows what it's like to have no food and then to overeat from a buffet. He has experienced both need and abundance. And he contends that you can be content with little or with a lot. How do we know this? Because he lived both and lived content no matter the circumstance he found himself in.

We have grown so accustomed to believing that in order for us to be content our circumstances have to change. Have you ever met a discontent wealthy person and a content poor person? Me too. Wealth and things don't determine contentment. The attitude of your heart does.

A few verses later Paul goes on to thank the church in Philippi for their generosity and the gift of money they have bestowed upon Paul during his time in prison under house arrest. Paul understood that the secret to contentment (even as he sat in prison) was gratitude.

Don't Forget to Remember

Gratitude opens the door to contentment. Without gratitude we could never take the losses of our life and see the blessings they can become. Gratitude is the action of grace. Grace is undeserved and unearned, and gratitude should be our response to the grace we receive from God. When we operate in gratitude, we begin to walk into contentment since we recognize that everything we have is from God and none of it was deserved. It's easy to be grateful and full of gratitude when life is going great, but what do we do when life isn't so easy?

Well, Paul would say, "Rejoice always, give thanks in all circumstances . . . for this is the will of God in Christ Jesus for you" (1 Thessalonians 5:16, 18).[4]

It can feel like more bad things have happened to us in our lives than good. But that's simply not the case. We just commonly forget all the things God has done for us and rehearse the negative moments of our life instead.

Paul could teach a master class on gratitude. He thanks the churches for their support, the leaders for their hospitality and grace; he thanks Jesus for this redemptive work. Paul knows something we don't. The more gratitude the less attitude. It is so easy to become critical of yourself, of others, and the world when you haven't stopped to be grateful.

In most of Paul's thirteen letters of the New Testament he's not giving the readers new information, he's reminding them of what they already know is true about Jesus. Paul and his counterparts already told them the message of Jesus, and they received it by faith. That's why they're in the various churches Paul writes to. They believed the gospel; they've just forgotten.

Life's circumstances will create temporary memory loss if we don't practice gratitude. Anyone can feel discontent with what they have when they forget to remember what they do have. It's easy to fall into that trap of feeling like you don't have what you need or want. Until you start rehearsing all the things God has provided for you. In the lonely seasons of singleness when I felt that what I had was not enough and all I wanted was more, I would start writing down all the things I did have.

I have good health.

I have a wonderful and supportive family.

I have my bachelor's degree and master's degree.

I have a beautiful home.

I have an incredible job with great benefits.

I have a strong community of friends.

I have fun life experiences and adventures.

I have all I need in Jesus.

If we look at culture, we will always feel like we need more. When we look at Jesus, we will know that we have more than enough.

Think About

- What would you be willing to lose to gain contentment? Paul was ready to give up his social network, his education, his reputation. How does that feel to you?
- What things in your life are you grateful for? Start a gratitude journal and make a list.

Chapter 10

Contentment Is My Home

They say there's no place like home. And they're right. I think we all recognize that "home" doesn't mean a house where you live.

Have you ever been a guest in someone else's home? It is so generous and thoughtful for a friend or family member to open their home to us to stay in. And although it's fun to have late-night chats reminiscent of middle school slumber parties, it's still not the same as sleeping in your own bed in your own home. It's all the unknowns in a house with which you're not familiar. Does the floor squeak when you have to get up in the middle of the night to use the restroom? Will the walk back to the guestroom cause the dog to wake up and start barking and wake up the house? Maybe it's better to lay awake all night with your bladder screaming at you than to take the risk of waking the house. And what's the waking-up protocol? Are you supposed to get up the same time they do or are you supposed to wait until they're done so you don't interrupt their morning routine? Sheesh. It's lovely, but it's awkward. It's off routine and out of sync with how you usually operate, no matter how homey your hospitable friends make it feel.

There is just no comparison to the feeling of home. Home is where you are your most honest, truest, and vulnerable self. It's the real you. Where you feel the greatest freedom. The greatest safety. The greatest belonging. And that's how contentment should feel. Like home.

I've lived in Idaho most of my life. And finding my way to the places that feel like home in my city requires no navigation, no need to consult a map. The streets are so familiar, the geography etched in my heart. Being here reminds me that reaching contentment is not like a destination on a journey. It's not a trendy Airbnb you pop into every once in a while for a hipster staycation. It's a home in which to live. Contentment is the place we were always designed to be. God created us to live in contentment, satisfied and fulfilled. How do I know this? Because it was the first home ever created, the Garden.

And the Lord God planted a garden in Eden, in the east, and there he put the man whom he had formed. And out of the ground the Lord God made to spring up every tree that is pleasant to the sight and good for food. The tree of life was in the midst of the garden, and the tree of the knowledge of good and evil. (Genesis 2:8–9)[1]

Everything we ever needed was in the Garden of Eden. Humanity was completely content. There was no lack. Nothing missing. Adam and Eve could find everything they ever desired in the garden. However, the serpent came in the garden to tell Eve she was missing something:

> Now the serpent was more crafty than any other beast of the field that the Lord God had made. He said to the woman, "Did God actually say, 'You shall not eat of any tree in the garden'?" (Genesis 3:1)[2]

Up until this moment in the garden, life was free of discontent.

There was no question where joy came from . . . the Creator.

There was no fear or anxiety about where your food or resources would come from.

There was no suffering, no shame.

There was no threat to risk.

There was no concern to wait.

There was no thought of wanting to be anywhere else than right where you were. I mean, what could be better than paradise?

There was complete satisfaction with what you had, no need for more.

You were completely satisfied and at home.

FOMO

Isn't it interesting how we never think we're missing something until someone tells us we are? FOMO—fear of missing out—has destroyed lives. Let's not even start on social media. I was happy with my computer mouse until I started seeing Instagram office posts with a millennial pink computer mouse, and all of a sudden even my computer equipment seemed lacking.

Eve was completely satisfied and content until the serpent told her she wasn't. Adam and Eve had everything they ever could have desired, but they made that mistake so many of us make; they bought into the idea that greater fulfillment was on the other side of obtaining just one more thing, eating from just one more tree, gaining just one more morsel of control.

They allowed the serpent to convince them there was a better place to live, a place in which they would have what was prohibited.

And ultimately, it was the one thing that was prohibited that drove them out of the garden and exiled them from home. The home where they were fully known and fully loved entirely in the actual presence of God. The home where fig leaves weren't required. The home where they could have stayed forever if they had embraced contentment instead of the lure of what Adam and Eve thought they were missing out on.

Do you know what the entire biblical narrative is really about? Getting us back home to Eden. To the place of total contentment. To the place of total satisfaction and fulfillment. Eden is home. Contentment is home.

The garden is the archetype for complete contentment. That's what God created us for. To live complete, lacking nothing in his garden paradise. Sin hijacked the plan and exiled us from the garden, and now humanity searches every day for home.

God's mission for the world is to get us back to the garden. We were made for contentment, not discontentment. Human sin and the evil in this world have every intention to keep us off the road to contentment. If the serpent can just keep us questioning, desiring more, unhappy, full of fear, ridden with shame from our suffering, always comparing ourselves, never satisfied . . . then he can detour our path.

And let's not miss this: Eden means "delight." And delight means "a high degree of satisfaction." That'll preach, now won't it? The very meaning of Eden, of home, is actually satisfaction, contentment. Eden as home, contentment as home, means that we can be delighted, no matter what swirls around us, no matter what comes at us. Because we are home.

David the psalmist even longs to get back to Eden when he writes,

How precious is your steadfast love, O God!
   The children of mankind take refuge in the shadow
      of your wings.
   They feast on the abundance of your house,

> and you give them drink from the river of your
> delights. (Psalm 36:7–8)[3]

The "river of your delights" is a reference to the Garden of Eden. It's a picture of an overflowing place of abundance, delight, pleasure . . . it's perfect contentment.

Let's kick it old school for a minute. Remember high school chemistry class? No, not just the hot guy who sat two seats in front of you and swept his hair casually back with a move oh-so-similar to Harry Styles. You may have done something called a litmus test back in that chem class, where you would test certain liquids to see if they were more acidic or alkaline. There are other kinds of litmus tests out there, for a variety of factors, and at their core, all litmus tests determine what, in terms of one factor, something is. In plain English, that means a litmus test is decisive.

You know what the litmus test for contentment is? Asking yourself whether your soul feels at home or not. That's it. The question, the test. So are you at home in your heart? Yes? Then that's contentment.

No? Then we've still got some work to do. Let's take a quick pause here and give ourselves a litmus contentment heart test, just a few questions to check for the conditions of our inner life.

What feels right in this season of your life?
What feels incomplete?

When you wake up in the morning, how would you describe the first thoughts that enter your mind? (Now, I'm not talking about how you feel waking up when you know you've got an awesome brunch date with that cute guy from four offices over. I'm not talking about how you feel after a particularly tough night of your six-month-old cutting a new tooth. I'm talking about what you would say is your general state on a typical morning. Choose from the following terms or jot down a few of your own: quietness, worry, anticipation, an immediate list of to-dos, dread, overwhelm, sadness, happiness, curiosity, fatigue, excitement.)

What is something you are most grateful for right now?

What is something you are most sad about right now?

Would you say your life at this point is right about on schedule for how you imagined it would be? Or does it seem to be hopelessly tardy on the things you were hoping to have in your life by now?

What feels familiar, recognizable in your life right now?

What feels unfamiliar, foreign, unsettling in your life?

As you're looking back over the things you wrote down and the phrases that you circled, what do you notice came easiest to you and flew from your pen the fastest? Did you write about the things you feel are missing or out of sequence or not matching your expectations? Or was it the things that you are grateful for, the things that you are finding joy and peace in? You should have found something to write in response to each of the questions above, because that's just life. As we talked about a couple of chapters ago, recognizing content-ment means that we know what discontent is as well. But those things that came to the top of your mind first, that's a great indicator of what's going on in your heart, a great litmus test to understand where you're truly living, where your home is, so to speak.

Not every season of life brings all the things I desire. My heart is still wanting. I still desire to be a mom, but until that season, I find myself at home in the chaos of my life . . . being a wife, an aunt, a daughter, a sister, and an author, a student, a preacher, a pastor, a friend.

Sometimes the way people talk about seasons in their lives makes it sound like home is something still on the hori-zon, something that won't be realized until the wedding hap-pens, the baby is born, the promotion or title is given. But home is not the exclusive sole and soul property of those with a marriage and a mortgage. I will never have enough time in this season to do all the things that are in my heart. Getting married and having children has never been my *only* dream; it's only part of the dream. So why not work on all the other parts while you can? I love studying and teaching the Bible. I love to equip and disciple leaders. I love to learn from books and take classes. I get to pour my heart out onto pages to hopefully encourage weary souls. I get to buy all the clothes I want because I'm not on a mom budget. (That day will come,

I know.) I get to watch a show in the middle of the day that I would like instead of watching *Blue's Clues*. I can work out without having to arrange childcare. Oops, did I slightly depress all the moms out there? Sorry, not my intention. Send me your babies, I'll babysit for a night. But see, there is a season for everything. I choose to enjoy every single season God has given me. And contentment in those seasons is home.

I'm perfectly content with what I have and what I don't have yet. Some would argue that sounds impossible, to be aware of what I don't have yet and yet still live in contentment. It's not about denying that there are still dreams in your heart that haven't come to pass yet. But we've got to be so careful not to confuse discontentment with vision. Great vision can drive us to do hard things, to wait with patience, to step out in faith, to let God lead actively. Vision is not about what we're missing. It's about living in a true joy as we look forward. Discontentment paralyzes us with a spirit of poverty, of deprivation.

The greatest challenge in living full-time at home in contentment is to fight the serpent's voice in our hearts trying to tell us there's something we're missing, hissing that what is missing means there's no way we could be content. Whenever the serpent sneaks into your thoughts, remind him and yourself, that the devil is a liar. God has given you absolutely everything you need right now to live at home in contentment. Whether you're a single woman waiting for marriage. Or one longing to hold a baby in your arms. Or a young mom longing for adult interaction again. Or a woman who feels she lost her identity being a wife and raising children. Or a grandmother who feels displaced. Every single season. Every single person. Every single story is right where God has you. He has equipped you with all you need to live this season well. Find your way back home to contentment.

So let's go back to that contentment litmus test for a moment. If you found that you were able to respond most quickly to those things in which you've found peace and trust and joy, that's great. Commit to staying in that frame of mind, even when circumstances shift, even when things go sideways. You've got a good window on what making a home of contentment should be like. But if you found it was much easier to define the elements of discontentment in your life, I want to encourage you to make use of your present season to help make contentment feel like home.

What are you saying about your season? Be intentional with what you are saying about your life. Now, listen, I'm not talking about not being honest about what's going on in your life. If your company just had layoffs and you were one of those handed a pink slip, I'm not saying contentment as your home means that you act like that's not a big deal or, even worse, refuse to process it and talk about it with trusted friends. What I'm saying is, if we are forever practicing discontentment by what we say, we're doomed to keep living it. If your narrative about your life is always about what is wrong, you can't hope to harvest contentment from that planting. Or if you are slapping up a paint of pessimism on the walls of your heart, it's going to color everything. So do a word inventory. If you have to, actually hit that voice memo function on your phone when you meet friends for coffee and record what you say. And then listen to it later. Take note of what you say, the words you use.

How often do phrases like "Well, if only this were different" or "It would be so much better if . . ." or "If only that person would notice me and my gifts . . . " or "If I could change this or that . . . " make it into your speech. Because here's the deal: The story you're repeating all the time to yourself becomes your story. Speaking contentment is a discipline. It sounds like "Yeah, I got a pink slip in that layoff. That was scary, and I'm not sure yet what all the ramifications of that are going to be. But I know God's got me. I know that He has equipped me for the next opportunity, and I know that if He allowed me to be removed from that position, then He's got something in mind that's going to be good I trust Him." That's honest contentment language. That's the kind of paint you want to put on the walls.

The Home Life of Paul

It's not lost on me that Paul never had a place to call home during his ministry. He started his entire experience with Jesus while on the road to Damascus, away from the familiar. And then he spent the rest of his earthly life in all kinds of places that weren't home in the sense we usually think of it. He was staying in other people's homes. He was staying in tents. Paul was staying in the hold of a ship as he was transported as a criminal of the state. He was constantly on missionary tour, traveling from new locale to new locale. He was staying in prison, under house arrest.

And yet he had such a firm grasp on making contentment about being with God, even to the point of finding complete peace in either staying on earth in his earthly body or taking the next train out of the mortal station. He wrote,

> For we live by faith, not by sight. We are confident, I say, and would prefer to be away from the body and at home with the Lord. So we make it our goal to please him, whether we are at home in the body or away from it. (2 Corinthians 5:7–9)[4]

Either way, Paul's aim to please God in his faith, his trust, his obedience, whether that means he is "housed," at home, in his physical body, or not.

Storing Up Treasures in Heaven, Not a Storage Unit

One of the booming industries in our country today is storage units. I was reading an article the other day that one in eleven Americans has at least one storage unit where they are putting all the extra stuff that won't fit in their house.[5] The article went on to explain that even with our bigger houses today, we've all fallen into the trap of getting more and more and more stuff. To be able to try to manage our homes, we've needed to get even more space. And so the storage unit market has now swelled to a cool $38 billion industry.

Our discontent and our need for more, more, more have pushed the limits of our homes beyond their capacity, and it has us out seeking even more space.

And then there's an even more interesting trend, one that gets highlighted in reality shows. People are struggling mightily with hoarding. It's estimated now in our country that 6 percent of our population, over 19 million Americans, are hoarders.[6] And I'm not talking about having a full house of mementos and an attic full of junk. It's the kind of hoarding that is debilitating, that makes the physical structure of a house dangerous for the occupants. It's the kind of hoarding that creates fire hazards and infestations. It's the kind of hoarding that prevents a house from being a home, because it is filled with the result of trauma and loss and discord, as the person hoarding seeks to comfort themselves with saving all the stuff that comes through their life.

What an apt metaphor for what we do to sabotage making contentment our home.

We want contentment. But we want other stuff, too. And we are comfortable with our stuff. The emotional stuff. The baggage. The collecting of hurts and uncertainties and our history. We gather up our grudges, and we pile them in the corners. We collect the garbage of the enemy's lies, and we scatter it across the counters. And we push in all the things we think we need to find happiness, and we cram in all the things that we think will protect us, and our discontent grows, and before we know it, we're digging through a storage unit of FOMO instead of resting at home in our hearts.

You've got things stored in your heart that are crowding out contentment. And you can't live in contentment, you can't make it your home, when there's so much *other* stuff competing for space.

I want you to visualize it, that place in your heart, in your mind, where *you*, the inner you, your soul, your essence, lives. I know it's a little meta but work with me here. What do you notice there? Do you see shards of past hurts always underfoot, ready to slice your heart? Do you see disappointment lurking over to the side, ready to slink in and make you sad? What if you did a spring cleaning of the soul?

What if you took those things out to the foot of the cross and just Let. Them. Go?

Jesus talks about this kind of cleaning of the heart, and He also gives a strong warning about being intentional about making sure our heart stays full of the right things. He says,

When an impure spirit comes out of a person, it goes through arid places seeking rest and does not find it. Then it says, "I will return to the house I left." When it arrives, it finds the house unoccupied, swept clean and put in order. Then it goes and takes with it seven other spirits more wicked than itself, and they go in and live there. And the final condition of that person is worse than the first. That is how it will be with this wicked generation. (Matthew 12:43–45)[7]

Friends, we've got to clear our hearts of the FOMO. And then we've got to cultivate contentment as our home. Otherwise, we're only moving out one form of discontent for another one to move in. I don't want to live moving from one state of discontentment to another. I want to live in consistent contentment! And I want that for you, too.

So it's time to sweep out the stuff. It's time to improve our definition of contentment, to make sure we aren't hoarding a flawed definition. It's time to chase joy, not just happiness. It's time to practice contentment even when storms are battering against the walls of our inner house. It's time to be honest about our struggles and to stop stockpiling shame. It's time to learn to wait well. It's time to be fully content with who God made us to be and with where He has placed us in this time and this season. It's time to simply follow where Jesus leads. It's time to be okay to let go, to lose those things that don't matter. It's time to stop renting space in what we think is that transient land of happy and to move home. Home to contentment. Jesus has fully paid the mortgage. He has handed you the keys, the wisdom of His word. Paul has modeled for you how to live in contentment well. And God will provide for you all you need when you live there, fully known, fully trusting, embracing that contentment as your Eden, the place where you walk with God.

Great Gain

We've traveled some choppy waters and rugged terrain together over the pages of this book, with our friend Paul. He showed us how to be okay with losing what we hold dear to follow Jesus wherever he leads us! Paul helped us to recognize the source and meaning of true joy. We can overcome thoughts of anxiety and fear by thinking of the right things. We may suffer—our friend Paul knows this better than anyone—but we do not have to live in the shame of our suffering. Paul shows us how to risk and not hide away in our safety boxes. We can joyfully wait because there's always movement in the waiting. Where we are right now is the best place we could possibly be! And it's probably the key to getting to the next place God has for us. And no matter what, we have all we need in Jesus, right now!

Near the end of Paul's life he writes a letter to his spiritual son, Timothy. He's getting old, gray, and perhaps realizing his days are numbered. The aging apostle writes,

> But godliness with contentment is great gain, for we brought nothing into the world, and we cannot take anything out of the world. But if we have food and clothing, with these we will be content. (1 Timothy 6:6–8).[8]

Paul learned that chasing after the glitz and glamour of life will never bring the satisfaction your soul longs for. Wealth without gratitude will only make us greedy, according to Paul. But the greatest gain is Jesus, our only true north, who leads us to Himself, the fulfiller of all contentment.

A few verses later Paul writes as if he expects to be with Jesus in paradise soon. He reminds his young student, Timothy, what really matters in this life and the one to come is the Creator of home.

> As for the rich in this present age, charge them not to be haughty, nor to set their hopes on the uncertainty of riches, but on God, who richly provides us with everything to enjoy. They are to do good, to be rich in good works, to be generous and ready to share, thus storing up treasure for themselves as a good foundation for the future, so that they may take hold of that which is truly life. (1 Timothy 6:17–19)[9]

You were made for contentment; it's always been your home.

Welcome home, my friend. Welcome home.

Acknowledgments

Garrison—thank you for loving me and being my greatest support (even through the stress of writing a book). You know how to make me laugh when I need it most and I can't imagine life without my best friend! I love you.

Mom and Dad (Connie and Ken)—thank you for always believing in me and for your continuous encouragement to pursue what is in my heart. Mom, you think of every detail and could probably run the world—instead, you're the greatest mom, intercessor, cheerleader, and friend. Dad, you raised me to believe that women can lead, preach, and teach, and I'm forever grateful for your belief in me. Love you both more than words can describe.

Krist and Kelly—your wisdom and support have always been a guide for me, and I'm thankful to have you as my pastors and siblings! Krist, you're the best big brother and will always be one of the most influencing voices in my life. Love you both.

Rachelle and Mark—thank you for walking alongside me through every season and always believing for God's best for my life and for always including me in the lonely seasons of my life. Rachelle, God gave me the most loving sister and best bosom buddy ever (cue Anne of Green Gables). Love you, guys.

Kenzington, Westley, Quincey, Whitney, Chloe, Kingsley, Presley, Waverley, and Riley—you nine have my heart and are the best blessings! Being your Aunt TT is one of the greatest joys of my life! Love you all sooooo much!

Jim and Tauni (Dad and Mom Pace)—thank you for welcoming me into your family as your own. I dreamed and prayed for in-laws just like you and God answered my every prayer. Love you.

Capital Church and Capital Young Adults—it is the greatest honor to serve Jesus alongside each of you. Thank you for your continuous prayers, support, and encouragement! I wouldn't be who I am without this wonderful community and family.

Esther and the entire team at the Fedd Agency—thank you for your diligent work on this project and for helping me share the message of contentment with as many people as possible.

Julie—to the wordsmith queen! Thank you for your input and help on this project. I couldn't have done it without you.

Team at Atria Books and Simon & Schuster—it truly takes a village to write a book and I'm grateful for all your effort, time, and support of this project.

Jesus—the archetype of contentment. Thank you for always leading the way!

Notes

Chapter 1: What Is Contentment? Already Not Yet

1. *The Holy Bible: English Standard Version.* Wheaton, IL: Crossway Bibles, 2016.
2. Ibid.
3. *The Holy Bible: New International Version.* Grand Rapids, MI: Zondervan, 1984.
4. *The Holy Bible: English Standard Version.* Wheaton, IL: Crossway Bibles, 2016.
5. *The Holy Bible: New International Version.* Grand Rapids, MI: Zondervan, 1984.
6. *The Holy Bible: English Standard Version.* Wheaton, IL: Crossway Bibles, 2016.
7. *The Holy Bible: The Message.* Colorado Springs, CO: NavPress, 2005.
8. *The Holy Bible: New International Version.* Grand Rapids, MI: Zondervan, 1984.

Chapter 2: Content to Follow Jesus

1. *The Holy Bible: English Standard Version.* Wheaton, IL: Crossway Bibles, 2016.
2. Ibid.
3. Ibid.
4. Ibid.
5. *The Holy Bible: New International Version.* Grand Rapids, MI: Zondervan, 1984.
6. *The Holy Bible: English Standard Version.* Wheaton, IL: Crossway Bibles, 2016.
7. Ibid.

Chapter 3: Content in Christian Joy: A Version of Happiness

1. *The Holy Bible: New International Version.* Grand Rapids, MI: Zondervan, 1984.
2. *The Holy Bible: English Standard Version.* Wheaton, IL: Crossway Bibles, 2016.
3. Ibid.
4. Ibid.

5 Ibid.
6 Ibid.
7 Ibid.
8 Ibid.
9 *The Holy Bible: New International Version*. Grand Rapids. MI: Zondervan, 1984.
10 Ibid.
11 *The Holy Bible: English Standard Version*. Wheaton, IL: Crossway Bibles, 2016.

Chapter 4: Content in Anxiety and Fear

1 https://www.theguardian.com/technology/2017/nov/09/facebook-sean-parker-vulnerability-brain-psychology
2 https://www.businessinsider.com/what-happens-to-your-brain-like-instagram-dopamine-2017-3
3 *The Holy Bible: New International Version*. Grand Rapids, MI: Zondervan, 1984.
4 *The Holy Bible: English Standard Version*. Wheaton, IL: Crossway Bibles, 2016.
5 Ibid.
6 *Holy Bible: New American Standard Bible*. LaHabra, CA: The Lockman Foundation, 1995.
7 *The Holy Bible: English Standard Version*. Wheaton, IL: Crossway Bibles, 2016.
8 Dr. Caroline Leaf, *Think, Learn, Succeed* (Kindle), p. 550.
9 Ibid., p. 435.
10 Ibid.
11 Ibid., p. 560.
12 *The Holy Bible: English Standard Version*. Wheaton, IL: Crossway Bibles, 2016.
13 E. H. Peterson, *A Long Obedience in the Same Direction: Discipleship in an Instant Society*. Downers Grove, IL: InterVarsity Press, 2000, p. 47.
14 *The Holy Bible: English Standard Version*. Wheaton, IL: Crossway Bibles, 2016.

Chapter 5: Content in Suffering and Shame

1 *Holy Bible: New English Translation*. (Ac 14:21–22) Biblical Studies Press, 2005.
2 *The Holy Bible: English Standard Version*. Wheaton, IL: Crossway Bibles, 2016.
3 Ibid.
4 C. S. Lewis, *The Problem of Pain*. New York: HarperCollins, 1945, p. 25.
5 Ibid.

6 Ibid., p. 20.
7 Ibid., p. 32.
8 Ibid.
9 *The Holy Bible: English Standard Version.* (Lk 8:40–56). Wheaton, IL: Crossway Bibles, 2016.
10 Ibid.
11 Dr. Rick Hanson, *Hardwiring Happiness: The New Brain Science of Contentment, Calm, and Confidence.* New York: Penguin Random House, 2013.
12 *The Holy Bible: English Standard Version.* Wheaton, IL: Crossway Bibles, 2016.
13 Ibid.

Chapter 6: Content to Risk over Safety

1 Scott Bader-Saye. *Following Jesus in a Culture of Fear.* Grand Rapids, MI: Brazos Press, 2017, p. 28.
2 Greg Lukianoff and Jonathan Haidt, *The Coddling of the American Mind: How Good Intentions and Bad Ideas Are Setting Up a Generation for Failure.* New York: Penguin Books, 2019, p. 30.
3 *The Holy Bible: English Standard Version.* Wheaton, IL: Crossway Bibles, 2016.
4 Ibid.
5 Ibid.
6 Ibid.
7 Ibid.
8 Ibid.
9 Ibid.
10 Ibid.
11 Ibid.

Chapter 7: Content to Wait

1 *The Holy Bible: English Standard Version.* Wheaton, IL: Crossway Bibles, 2016.
2 *The Holy Bible: New International Version.* Grand Rapids, MI: Zondervan, 1984.
3 Ibid.
4 Ibid.
5 Ibid.
6 Ibid.

Chapter 8: Content in Where I Am

1 *The Holy Bible: New International Version.* Grand Rapids, MI: Zondervan, 2011.

2 *Holy Bible: New Living Translation.* Wheaton, IL: Tyndale House Publishers, 2004.
3 *The Holy Bible: English Standard Version.* Wheaton, IL: Crossway Bibles, 2016.
4 *The Holy Bible: New International Version.* Grand Rapids, MI: Zondervan, 2011.
5 *The Holy Bible: English Standard Version.* Wheaton, IL: Crossway Bibles, 2016.

Chapter 9: Content with What I Have

1 *The Holy Bible: English Standard Version.* Wheaton, IL: Crossway Bibles, 2016.
2 Ibid.
3 Ibid.
4 Ibid.

Chapter 10: Contentment Is My Home

1 *The Holy Bible: English Standard Version.* Wheaton, IL: Crossway Bibles, 2016.
2 Ibid.
3 Ibid.
4 *The Holy Bible: New International Version.* Grand Rapids, MI: Zondervan, 2011.
5 https://www.curbed.com/2018/3/27/17168088/cheap-storage-warehouse-self-storage-real-estate
6 https://www.washingtonpost.com/national/health-science/hoarding-is-serious-disorder—and-its-only-getting-worse-in-the-us/2016/04/11/b64a0790-f689-11e5-9804-537defcc3cf6_story.html?noredirect=on&utm_term=.a65d39ed14d9
7 *The Holy Bible: New International Version.* Grand Rapids, MI: Zondervan, 2011.
8 *The Holy Bible: English Standard Version.* Wheaton, IL: Crossway Bibles, 2016.
9 Ibid.

This page constitutes a continuation of the copyright page:

About the Author

Tracy Wilde-Pace is wife to Garrison and soon-to-be mom to their first child. She is an executive pastor at Capital Church as well as the college and young adult pastor of Capital Young Adults in Boise, Idaho. Tracy received her bachelor's degree in political science from Northwest Nazarene University in Nampa, Idaho, and her master's of divinity (MDiv) in practical theology from Regent University in Virginia Beach, Virginia.

Tracy and her husband, Garrison, live in beautiful Boise, Idaho, where they both grew up.

She is also the author of *Finding the Lost Art of Empathy*. Tracy speaks both nationally and internationally, where she loves talking about Jesus and the Bible.

Twitter: www.twitter.com/tracywilde
Instagram: www.instagram.com/tracywilde
www.tracywilde.com
www.capitalchurch.com